PLANTS & GARDENS

BROOKLYN BOTANIC GARDEN RECORD

PRUNING
TECHNIQUES

1991

Brooklyn Botanic Garden

STAFF FOR THIS EDITION:

ALAN D. COOK, GUEST EDITOR

BARBARA B. PESCH, DIRECTOR OF PUBLICATIONS

JANET MARINELLI, ASSOCIATE EDITOR

AND THE EDITORIAL COMMITTEE OF THE BROOKLYN BOTANIC GARDEN

BEKKA LINDSTROM, ART DIRECTOR

JUDITH D. ZUK, PRESIDENT, BROOKLYN BOTANIC GARDEN

ELIZABETH SCHOLTZ, DIRECTOR EMERITUS, BROOKLYN BOTANIC GARDEN

STEPHEN K-M. TIM, VICE PRESIDENT, SCIENCE & PUBLICATIONS

COVER PHOTOGRAPH BY CHRISTINE M. DOUGLAS

Plants & Gardens, Brooklyn Botanic Garden Record (ISSN 0362-5850) is published quarterly at 1000 Washington Ave., Brooklyn, N.Y. 11225, by the **Brooklyn Botanic Garden, Inc.** Second-class-postage paid at Brooklyn, N.Y., and at additional mailing offices. Subscription included in Botanic Garden membership dues ($25.00) per year.

ISBN # 0-945352-61-1

PLANTS & GARDENS

BROOKLYN BOTANIC GARDEN RECORD

PRUNING TECHNIQUES

VOL. 47, NO. 1*, SPRING 1991

HANDBOOK # 126

*PLEASE NOTE: To make all four issues of each volume of *Plants & Gardens* appear in the same calendar year, we've renumbered this issue. This issue replaces Vol. 46 No. 4.

FOREWORD

Plants are vital to both our physical and mental health. Plants also can increase property values significantly — if, that is, they're properly pruned for beauty and bounty, vigor and longevity.

Unfortunately, proper pruning is perhaps the least understood of all human endeavors.

Paint peels; cars won't run; dresses don't fit; your prescription is for hangnails instead of gout...Most folks immediately recognize that the painter, mechanic, dressmaker or physician has goofed.

But an untrained tree worker mutilates a 200-year-old oak; a homemaker shears all shrubs and small trees into gumdrops; a mower scalps bluegrass thin as a cheap bath towel. And yet most folks, it sadly seems, view such reprehensible work with misguided appreciation.

Basic proper pruning is not instinctive. It must be learned, just like basic proper painting, auto repair, dressmaking and medicine. This handbook is intended to provide basic knowhow; we've included a glossary to make learning proper pruning technique as simple as possible. Give it a try.

Yet pruning can be more than just "basic" and "proper." Transcendent proper pruning adds an element of artistry; an element not essential for plant health and function, but essential to the ultimate aesthetic touch.

Possibly, this handbook, in addition to giving the basics, will awaken your latent artistic pruning talents. Give this a chance, too.

ALAN D. COOK
GUEST EDITOR

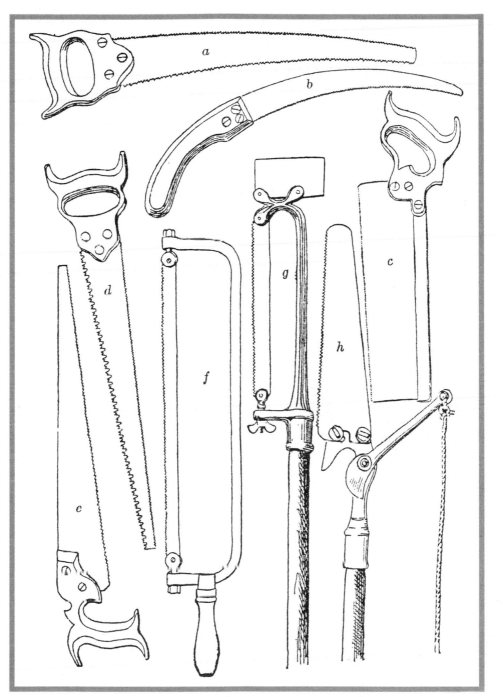

An assortment of antique pruning tools.

This lacebark pine, *Pinus bungeana*, has been pruned to expose the attractive bark.

REASONS
&
SEASONS
FOR
PRUNING

ALAN D. COOK

Pruning is the removal of a part or parts, living or dead, of a living plant. There are several reasons for pruning, including the following:

❶ To maintain the "natural" appearance of a plant. Sometimes this enhances, sometimes it defies, a plant's natural tendencies. (An old nurseryman once remarked, "We have to prune the dickens out of this variety to keep it looking natural.") This can include striving for natural appearance in extreme miniature, as in bonsai.

❷ To create and maintain an unnatural

ALAN D. COOK, *Director of Extended Services at the Dawes Arboretum in Newark, Ohio, is the Guest Editor of this handbook.*

appearance of a plant. Examples are sheared hedges, sheared individual plants (gumdrops) poodle-tailed shrubs, topiary figures, espaliers, pollarding and pleaching.

❸ To limit the size of a plant (keep it "in bounds").

❹ To enhance plant health by removing dead, badly damaged, diseased and/or insect-infested parts of plants.

❺ To improve plant structure (and thus enhance health), especially trees and large shrubs, by removing crowded branches, crossing branches, branches with narrow (weak) crotch angles and shoots in competition with main leaders.

❻ To remove undesirable growth that detracts from a plant — especially suckers and watersprouts.

❼ To display attractive bark on trees and large shrubs by pruning off some lower branches.

❽ To maximize attractive bark on smaller shrubs by cutting back severely during dormancy to promote strong new shoots annually.

❾ To improve or maintain flowering by removing spent flowers, especially on flowering plants which do not have attractive fruit, such as lilacs, rhododendrons and many herbaceous plants.

❿ To improve or maintain fruiting (especially edible fruits).

⓫ To rejuvenate old shrubs.

⓬ To increase safety to humans by removing branches that obstruct traffic signs and signals, oncoming traffic and so on.

⓭ To remove limbs that might fall on people and property.

⓮ To remove low-hanging limbs, protruding thorny branches and other plant conditions that pose hazards to human motion on foot or by vehicle.

⓯ To obtain materials for decorative purposes, such as floral arrangements and holiday decorations.

Seasons for Pruning

In some areas, recommended pruning seasons for certain species may be influenced by possible insect and/or disease problems. White oaks, for example, in some areas may be susceptible to oak wilt disease if pruned prior to summer. Check with local authorities.

Winter is a good time for arborists to prune large trees, and for nonprofessionals to prune shrubs and small trees. The absence of deciduous foliage at this time of year helps make the material to be pruned more visible and reduces cleanup chores. More specifically, early spring, before new growth (including swelling of buds), is the best time for this kind of pruning . Early spring also is the best time for severe rejuvenation pruning of shrubs (see "Pruning Deciduous and Needled Evergreen Shrubs," page 36), including shrubs with colorful bark for beauty next fall and winter.

Some trees, including maples, birches, walnut, dogwood and fruit trees, "bleed" sap profusely if pruned in early spring. This is unsightly but causes little or no harm to the trees. If such a tree needs serious pruning, a temporary aesthetic setback is a small price to pay.

Roses and other summer-blooming shrubs respond well to early spring pruning.

In general, pruning in early spring promotes vigorous new growth. On the other hand, response to pruning during the period of new growth later in spring is poor, because food reserves in roots and stems are low at this time. Avoid extensive pruning, such as cutting to the ground for rejuvenation, during this period of burgeoning new growth. Heavy pruning at this time weakens plants, sometimes fatally; pruning should be minimal — for example, to remove a broken branch.

Late spring is the time-honored season for pruning spring-flowering shrubs and trees — that is, after they blossom — because the floral display is least impaired. However, if the plants are overgrown and densely twiggy, a good pruning job in early spring may be best in the long run.

Response to summer pruning is much less vigorous than to early spring pruning. Thus, summer is the season to remove suckers and watersprouts, and to do pruning aimed at keeping plants in bounds, because growth response is moderate. Avoid severe pruning, especially of weak plants, in summer.

Hedges and topiaries are good candidates for summer pruning, as are shrubs in foundation plantings. Summer pruning of fruit trees is useful to minimize rank growth that can complicate harvest.

Fall pruning is usually confined to removal of diseased and insect-ridden parts and dead wood. Vigorous fall pruning of woody plants may result in new growth which hasn't had enough time to harden before winter. Especially vulnerable to freeze damage due to late pruning are roses, azaleas and hollies, especially plants of borderline hardiness in a given zone.

Of course, fall is the time to cut back herbaceous perennials, except those of evergreen persuasion.

PRUNING TREES

R. A. BARTLETT

Pruning shade and ornamental trees involves the removal of dead, dying, diseased, damaged, insect infested and/or superfluous branches. (It also involves severing roots for various reasons, a subject covered elsewhere in this handbook.) What follows is an overview of pruning the above-ground portions of trees.

General Rules

Don't prune without first considering its effect on the overall physiology of the tree. It is easy to weaken a tree by employing improper techniques, by removing too much at one time and/or by pruning at the wrong time of year.

R.A. BARTLETT *is Chairman of the Board of Directors of F.A. Bartlett Tree Expert Company in Stamford, Connecticut. He was instrumental in the establishment of Bartlett Arboretum at the University of Connecticut.*

9

Cut dead branches as close to the living branch collar as possible. Do not injure living tissue.

If you cut too close, wound-wood will not form properly, providing an entry for decay organisms.

Branch collars are large on some trees as shown here. Sizes can vary even on the same tree.

Each pruning cut must be made correctly with an appropriate tool, recently sharpened and in good operating order.

As a rule of thumb, do not remove more than one-fourth of the live branches at one time, or more than one-third in one year. Removal of greater amounts of a tree canopy will reduce photosynthetic capacity and deprive the tree of sufficient food for healthy growth. Removal of large amounts of foliage also exposes the inner bark of thin-barked trees, inviting sunscald.

As for timing, see "When to Prune," below.

Reasons to Prune

The primary reasons to prune trees include safety, sanitation and health, enhancement of character and beauty, guidance or restriction of future growth and opening up a view or views.

Codominant stems grow at the same rate from the same point, making a fork — without a branch collar.

The stem bark ridge is the key to pruning one of two codominant stems. Do not leave stubs.

Safety is the most widely recognized reason to prune trees. Branches that are likely to fall or break should be lightened or completely removed, unless they can be supported. Dense crowns that catch wind like a sail should be thinned to enable strong winds to pass harmlessly through.

Young trees should be trained not only so that they assume the characteristic silhouette of their species, but to eliminate future weak junctures of branches and trunks.

Sanitation pruning means the removal of dead and dying branches and of insect-infested and diseased wood. Suckers (upright shoots from the base) and watersprouts (upright shoots arising from branches) should be removed to divert the plant's energy toward desirable branches and strong overall growth.

Thinning a dense crown allows light and air to penetrate, which reduces the

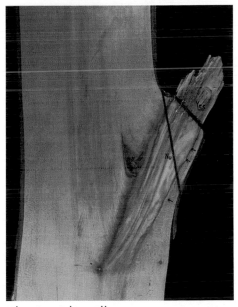

The "no" line illustrates an improper cut. For proper wound closing, cut along the "yes" line.

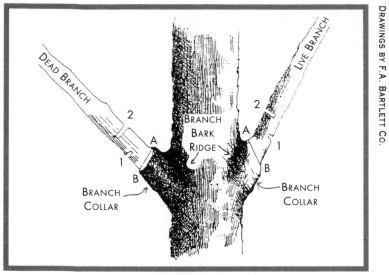

DRAWINGS BY F.A. BARTLETT CO.

Hardwood

possibility of insect and disease problems, while also reducing the tree's demands for water and nutrients during periods of stress.

Space restrictions (trees planted too close together or too close to structures, rights-of-way or utility wires) tax the skill and artistry of arborists. In some cases, such as beneath wires, it is better to remove a tall- and fast-growing species and replace it with a more suitable tree.

Pruning for vistas is popular where trees block views of mountains, water scenes and the like. However, it takes considerable skill to open "windows" for the enjoyment of such splendor without disfiguring the trees.

A Word of Warning

Before describing some basic pruning techniques, I should emphasize that gardeners should not prune trees without proper training and full use of safety equipment.

Never attempt to prune trees from a ladder. Keep both feet firmly on the ground, and never prune any heavy branches higher than your shoulders. If it is necessary to leave the ground to prune, call in a professional.

Basic Tree Pruning Techniques

When removing branches, alive or dead, be careful not to cut or otherwise injure the branch collar, the bulge of growth on the trunk at the base of the branch. (See drawing.)

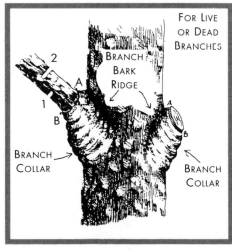

Conifer

REMOVING LARGE LIMBS

Let's define a large limb as one you cannot hold easily in one hand when you sever it from a tree with a saw in the other hand. Experience quickly demonstrates that a large limb, thus defined, is not all that large.

The way to remove a large limb, without tearing bark and even wood that should have been left intact, is by the three-cut method.

First, make a cut about a foot away from the point of attachment on the trunk (or larger branch) of the branch to be removed; cut from the bottom, about one-third of the way through the limb, or until the saw starts to bind as weight of the branch squeezes the kerf.

Then, about two inches farther out, cut through the branch so it falls away, leaving a stub. This technique is called a "drop cut," and should result in the branch dropping more or less straight downward.

The third cut removes the stub just outside the branch collar at the proper angle (equal to and opposite from the angle of the branch bark ridge).

A "jump cut" begins with the first cut made as described above. The second cut is made about two inches closer to the trunk. The cut end of the branch should spring up and away as it falls.

Then proceed with the third and final cut as described above. (See sketches.)

Note the use of "should" in both procedural descriptions above. Be ready for anything — always — when cutting large limbs.

If the branch collar is indistinct, make the removal cut at an angle equal to but opposite that made by the branch bark ridge, the darker ridge of bark which forms above the intersection of trunk and branch. (See drawing.)

All but the smallest branches require a series of three cuts (as shown in the drawing). The first is an undercut made from six to twelve inches out from the trunk, and one-third or more of the way through the branch. (If your saw begins to bind, you've cut far enough.)

The second cut is downward, about three inches farther out on the branch from the undercut. Continue this cut until the branch falls away. Heavy branches that are apt to damage lower branches or something on the ground should be secured by a rope or two prior to the first cut, and lowered safely after the second cut.

The third (and final) cut starts at the top, just outside the branch bark ridge, and should be angled slightly away from the trunk to remove the branch without damaging the branch collar. Never leave a stub, or make a flush cut. Both will prevent proper closing of the wound, and will provide easy entry for insects and disease organisms.

Do not paint or coat the pruning wound, with the possible exception of a thin coat for cosmetic purposes. Years ago, painting was a revered practice. Today we know it serves no useful purpose and in some cases can even hold in moisture and foster decay.

Small branches, suckers, watersprouts and ends of conifer branches can be removed with a single cut with a sharp handsaw, pole pruner, pole saw or hand shears.

It is unwise for nonprofessionals to use chain saws and/or flexible chain devices on cords advertised for cutting overhead branches.

When to Prune

Trees can be pruned at any time of the year, with one exception—severe pruning (removal of more than one-fourth of the crown at one time) should not be done in early summer, when food reserves in trunks and roots are low.

PLASTIC BANDAGES FOR TREE WOUNDS

So paint does not help tree wounds. Then what can we do?

For sizable wounds on tree trunks, such as those caused all too often by car fenders and bumpers, wound closing can be aided by black plastic bandages thick enough to exclude light.

If applied soon (within two weeks, tops) after the wound was inflicted, 4-mil black plastic, or several layers of thinner material, will speed wound closing and reduce decay of exposed wood, according to research by Drs. Alex Shigo and Walter Shortle of United States Department of Agriculture Division of Forestry.

Applied more than two weeks later, the plastic bandage will reduce decay, but not accelerate wound closing.

One arborist in Ohio has used black plastic electrical tape, wrapped completely around the tree trunk at top, middle and bottom, to effectively secure the "bandage."

After one year, the bandage should be removed.

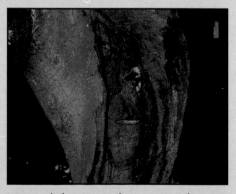

Wound dressings do not stop decay — some dressings encourage it.

TOPLESS TREES ARE INDECENT

Topping destroys a tree's beauty and shortens its life.

If a tree is growing too large for a given site, it's the fault of the person who planted it there. Proper pruning can help allay the size problem, especially if started early in the life of the tree.

Topping does not solve the size problem. But it does create new problems.

The immediate result of truncating a trunk or large limb is either dieback or prolific vigorous upright shoots from below the cut, forming a "broom."

These new shoots arise from just under the bark and thus are poorly attached and easily broken off by wind.

Indeed, a few years after topping, not only may a tree be as tall as before, but density of branches and foliage may even be greater. Consequently, there's more wind resistance, and the entire tree is more vulnerable to breakage or uprooting.

The monetary value of a tree, and thus of the entire property on which it grows, is reduced by topping.

Life expectancy of the tree is lowered, usually by at least one-third. Stressed, weakened trees may die a year or two after topping.

However, perhaps the greatest insult of the topping crime is the loss of a tree's beauty, majesty and dignity.

Before pruning.

A few trees bleed (ooze sap) when pruned in late winter and early spring, but this is more unsightly than harmful. Trees that bleed readily include maples, birches, black walnut and flowering dogwood.

Trees that flower in spring should be pruned immediately after flowering, so that next year's flowering is not reduced.

Trees damaged by storms should be pruned as soon as possible after the dam-

After pruning.

age, to induce wound-covering new growth without delay.

Winter pruning makes it easier to see the proper locations to prune, since at this time of year they are not obscured by foliage. Winter pruning also is usually faster and less costly because fewer precautions are required to avoid damage to lawns and gardens, and cleanup is easier without leaves.

HOW TO HIRE A TREE-CARE PRO

STEVE SANDFORT & EDWIN C. BUTCHER

You hear a knock on the door. The person standing there explains that his tree company is in the neighborhood and he noticed a problem with your tree. He says he does good work at a low price; he might even show you a business card claiming he is "Fully Insured." Should you authorize him to work on your trees? If you do, both you and your trees stand a good chance of getting the clipping of your lives.

According to numerous studies, your landscaping — especially trees — can contribute up to 20 percent of your property value. Rather than paying a fly-by-night tree service to mutilate (one of the authors would rather not use the word "butcher"!) your trees, you'll be dollars ahead if you hire a professional tree service. You get what you pay for!

Most homeowners fail to look up at their trees. You should regularly look for dead limbs, discolored leaves, leaves that are smaller and/or more sparse than normal. These symptoms usually indicate problems

How do you select a professional tree service? That can be difficult. The Cincinnati Yellow Pages lists about 65 tree-service companies, and there are probably another 65 unlisted ones cruising the area. It is a well-known fact that as unemployment increases, so does the number of tree "experts."

A general rule of thumb is that good, reputable tree-service companies do not need to solicit business door-to-door. They stay busy with repeat customers or recommendations from satisfied clients. Professional tree companies report about six weeks of backlog in summer and two weeks in winter. With this much work, there's simply no time to solicit door to door.

Call a tree service recommended by several of your friends or neighbors. Some cities have a local Arborists Association that you can call for recommendations. Usually only the better companies are members.

If no one can recommend a company, look in your Yellow Pages under "Trees." The better companies are members of one or two professional organizations.

The National Arborist Association restricts membership only to tree-service companies whose work is of high quality and ethical standards.

EDWIN C. BUTCHER *is founder and president of Madison Tree Service in Cincinnati. He is a former Associate Professor of Arboriculture at Cincinnati Technical College, and has given talks on arboriculture to professional groups in the U.S. and abroad.*

STEVE SANDFORT *is Supervisor of Urban Forestry for the City of Cincinnati, Ohio. In addition to running an exemplary urban forestry department, Sandfort has authored an award-winning tree book for the general public and numerous articles for professional journals.*

PHOTO COURTESY OF DAVEY TREE EXPERT COMPANY, KENT, OHIO.

Most good tree-service companies have clean,
modern equipment.

Membership in the International Society of Arboriculture is open to individuals practicing tree work or working in a closely related field — forestry, research, teaching or managing tree-covered cemeteries, campuses or arboreta.

Member companies of either of these organizations and/or their local chapters are usually up to date on theories and methods of tree care. However, as with members of any profession, arborists may offer differing opinions of what is wrong with your tree and how to treat it. Therefore, it is always wise to get a second or third opinion from other tree companies, especially if a large sum of money is involved, or if the tree in question is extremely valuable.

In many areas, there are competent individuals who do not sell or perform any tree-service work but who, for a fee, will consult with you about your tree problem. Many of these private consultants belong to the American Society of Consulting Arborists. Quite often city foresters, electric utility foresters or similar professionals perform consulting services in their off-time. Consultants can provide you with unbiased opinions and later check the work for quality and completeness before you pay the bill.

Most good tree-service companies have clean, modern equipment that is kept in good repair. Their employees are generally neat and polite. Reputable companies provide all types of tree care including pruning, fertilizing, mulching, cabling and bracing, lightning protection and pest control.

The professional approach is to first try to save the tree, and to recommend removal only as a last resort (especially if a tree poses danger to life and property). If a tree's problem is not serious and needs no treatment, they will even tell you that!

Never will a good company use boot spikes (gaffs) to climb a tree that is to remain in your landscape. Using spikes is in direct conflict with all arboricultural standards.

Only on rare occasions do reputable companies recommend or perform topping of trees. What would you think of a marine biologist who advocated chopping the tails off whales because whales get too long? Look around your city and see how many homeowners have fallen prey to the old snake-oil line that goes: "We'll top your tree because it's getting too tall."

Trees are supposed to be tall. Topping (pollarding, stubbing off, hatracking, dehorning) is almost never recommended unless a tree has suffered drastic damage from, for example, a tornado or plane crash. Then the cuts are made to minimize further death or rot in remaining branches.

Routine topping, as advocated by the quacks of the tree-service industry, usually results in dead trees or large truncated branches that cannot callus over their horrible wounds. These huge stubs begin to rot while small sucker sprouts begin to grow around the edges. As the rot gets more serious, the sprouts get heavier and finally crash to the ground when the rotted wood can no longer support their weight.

Topping a tree ruins its natural beauty and severely shortens its life expectancy. Severe topping of a tree already under stress, and/or at a time when carbohydrate reserves are low (late spring, early summer) may result in almost immediate death.

If a company advertises topping or suggests doing it to your tree, consider that company no further. If it is necessary to reduce the weight or size of the top of a large tree, a good arborist can prune 50 percent of the wood out so that only a skilled eye will be able to detect that the tree was even pruned. This type of professional pruning leaves a tree looking like the beautiful creation it is and greatly extends the tree's life by eliminating dead, weak, diseased, splitting or rubbing branches.

Before allowing a tree-service company to work on your property, obtain copies of the company's certificates of insurance and workman's compensation (or the equivalent in your state). Do not rely on the company's business card or Yellow Page ad claiming it is "fully insured."

A certificate of insurance looks much like the single sheet you receive from your automobile insurance company explaining the limits of your liability, collision and medical coverage. This certificate proves that the tree-service company is insured in the event its activities damage your property. Damage can range from a crushed shrub to a totally smashed house, but if the company is insured, its insurance will pay.

Before the work starts, phone the insurance carrier to make certain that your chosen tree service is still covered.

State workman's compensation pays the medical and long-term disability costs of any tree-service-company employee who is injured on the job. Remember, tree work is highly hazardous. In some states, if an injured employee of a company without workman's compensation cannot get enough money from his employer to pay medical bills, that worker can then turn to the property owner for compensation.

Some property owners think their homeowner insurance will cover them in such a case, but not all homeowner policies do. If they do, the maximum limit is far less than the amount for which the injured worker may sue you.

The fly-by-night tree "expert" will most likely quote you a cheaper price for the work than will a reputable company, but remember, you get what you pay for. Paying for liability and workman's compensation insurance is very expensive, and only the best, most professional companies carry sufficient insurance. It costs over $100,000 to initially hire, equip, train and insure a three-man crew and at least $80,000 per year to keep a tree service going thereafter. These costs, plus the costs of memberships in and technical training sponsored by professional organizations, all have to be built into prices charged by good tree services.

Though it is wise to get more than one estimate, you should not expect good tree-service companies to engage in a bidding war. Most have established hourly rates, and sound estimates are based on those rates

Once you decide on the company, the type of work to be done and what it will cost, get all your promises in writing. The good companies will submit a proposal that states:

● What date the work will begin.
● Exactly what work will be done. For example, prune all dead, dying, diseased and weak branches one and one half inches or greater in diameter.
● What you need to do, such as remove lawn furniture, keep children and pets indoors, etc.
● What cleanup work will be done and when. Do you keep the wood, and if so, how will it be left — cut into 16 inch lengths and stacked by the garage? Does the removal of a tree include grinding out the stump and surface roots to one foot below grade, replacing all chips with topsoil and then sowing grass seed? Unless otherwise specified, most estimates are based on removal to near ground

level and not grinding the stump.
● What date the work will be finished.
● The total dollar amount you will be charged. This is important in order to avoid misunderstandings such as:

"Here is the $300 I owe you for my five trees."

"$300? Sorry, lady, that was $300 per tree!

Never pay in advance. All good companies will bill you, but you should pay that bill promptly if the company performed properly. If there is a problem, immediately call it to the attention of the company's sales representative or president. Don't pay until all the work and any necessary corrections are done to your satisfaction or that of your consultant.

Another tree mendous tip to consider in obtaining the most cost-effective tree work is to schedule as much work as possible for the winter months. Most tree work can be done as well or better in the winter. However, few people think about their trees then, so it is usually a slow season for tree services. Quite often companies will offer slightly better rates to encourage off-season work.

In addition, see if any of your neighbors have been thinking about having tree work done; then get bids from several reputable companies for all the work at the same time. Combined with lower winter rates, group discounts can result in savings of 10 to 15 percent!

Your shade trees are nice to have around! There are a lot of folks willing to put a chainsaw to them for a fast buck. There are also professional companies whose reputations talk for them.

Allowing the wrong company to work on your trees can turn out to be a costly mistake. Don't let it happen to you. Using your common sense and the helpful hints outlined here will almost guarantee that cost-effective, quality tree work is performed on your property with little risk to you or your trees. ❦

PRUNING ROOTS

ALAN D. COOK

Four kinds of root pruning are discussed here: pruning girdling roots, pruning raised roots, pruning to reduce a plant's vigor or growth and pruning before transplanting.

Girdling Roots

Sometimes a misguided root grows at right angles to the radial direction of normal roots. If this happens close to the trunk, girdling (squeezing) can occur as trunk and root expand with time. Trunk expansion is then reduced, sometimes severely, causing eventual flattening of the trunk above the girdle. In severe cases, this can result in severe loss of tree vigor.

This unhappy condition occurs among trees grown too long in round containers in nurseries, leading to circular root growth. And sometimes trees transplanted bare-root will produce girdling roots, especially if roots are forced into an undersized transplanting hole. Maples, especially Norway maple, *Acer platanoides*, seem prone to girdling roots.

Girdling roots should be cut away as soon as you see them, as close to their points of origin as possible. Considerable soil removal may be necessary to expose the girdler.

Saws are often awkward to use in constricted spaces, and moving contact with soil will dull saw teeth rapidly. Sometimes a sharp axe is appropriate, but usually a hammer and chisel work best.

Raised Roots

Many tree and some shrub species generate raised roots, especially in heavy soils. Mowing and walking over exposed roots are not much fun. Mulching and use of groundcovers are possible solutions, but sometimes you just want to get rid of the offending root(s).

Pruning exposed roots may be accomplished as discussed above for girdling roots.

Vigorous trees will suffer little harm if a few raised roots are cut and removed. However, removing roots from trees under stress is not wise. There seems to be no formula for the amount of roots a tree can lose without undue harm. So practice restraint.

Root Pruning for Vigor Reduction

Cutting roots reduces vigor of a plant to some degree, and is most often done

on shrubs. A rampant shrub may be
kept in bounds by root pruning, especially if judicious thinning and heading back of branches are done at the
same time.

The job is more or less easily accomplished by thrusting a straight-bladed
spade vertically into the soil at points
between stem-root juncture and drip line
(edge of branch spread).

As with removal of raised roots,
undue enthusiasm is not recommended.

Pre-Transplant Root Pruning

Pruning roots of a sizable shrub or tree
one growing season before transplanting
was a common practice years ago. Generally, a trench was dug around the woody
plant at about the radius of the proposed
transplanting root ball, and about 18
inches deep.

Some practioners used an interrupted
trench. Then soil, usually amended with
organic material such as humus or peat
moss, was replaced. The next season,
new roots were expected to have formed
in fibrous profusion, increasing the
chances for a successful transplant.

This procedure is seldom practiced by
professional nursery people today. 🌼

PETER NELSON

Girdling roots can be above or below
ground. If flattening of the trunk or
loss of vigor is noted, start digging.

TRAINING & PRUNING FRUIT TREES

Marcia Eames-Sheavly & Marvin P. Pritts

During nonbearing early years, fruit trees need some pruning. The emphasis should be on training for tree structure. Special attention should be given to selecting limbs that are well spaced along the trunk of the tree and that have wide angles of attachment. The development of a structurally strong tree with limbs well exposed to full sunlight will greatly reduce the amount of corrective pruning needed during the production years.

Figures 1 through 6 illustrate the principles of pruning.

Apples and Pears

Apple and pear trees should be pruned during the dormant season, which is after leaves have fallen and before growth starts in the spring. The ideal pruning time in New York State is from February to April.

Pruning cuts on young trees stimulate vegetative growth and delay fruit bearing. Therefore, keep the number of cuts on a nonbearing tree to a minimum, making only those necessary for proper structural development.

At planting, cut back one-year-old unbranched trees to a height of 24 to 30 inches. After new shoots start to grow, remove the second and third shoots from the top to avert narrow-angled crotch development of the permanent scaffold limbs.

When planting a two-year-old branched tree, select a leader branch and three or four well spaced lateral branches for the permanent framework, and remove the other branches. After growth begins, remove the second and third new shoots from the tip of the leader.

Training during the second year depends upon the growth habit of the cultivar. If the cultivar tends naturally to be a spreading tree such as Golden Delicious, remove only the crowding shoots.

Also remove fruits that set on the leader. If fruits are allowed to develop on the leader, it is not possible to maintain the upright position necessary for a

MARCIA EAMES-SHEAVLY *received her bachelor's degree in horticulture from Cornell University. After a stint as a Cooperative Extension agent, she returned to Cornell as a technician in the Department of Fruit and Vegetable Science.*
MARVIN PRITTS *received his doctorate at Michigan State University and does teaching, research and extension work in the Department of Fruit and Vegetable Science at Cornell.*

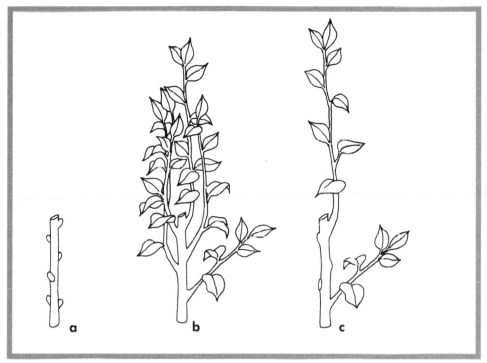

Fig. 1 SUMMER PRUNING OF YOUNG TREE TO ENSURE DOMINANCE OF THE LEADER:
a) head back the unbranched whip at planting;
b) vigorous shoots develop from the uppermost buds;
c) remove shoots that compete with the leader while the plant is still succu-
lent; continue the removal of competing shoots in subsequent years.

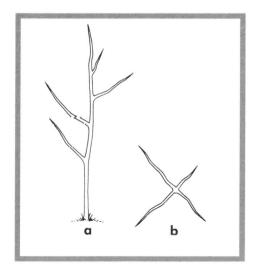

Fig. 2 PRINCIPLES OF
SCAFFOLD SELECTION AND TRAINING:
a) a tier of "scaffold limbs" or principal branches that form the tree's
framework should be well spaced
along the trunk, with no more than
one scaffold arising from any point;
the first should be at least 18 inches
from the ground;
b) the tree as viewed from above;
note good distribution of scaffolds;
keep upper scaffolds smaller than
lower scaffolds to maintain proper
light exposure of lower scaffolds.

   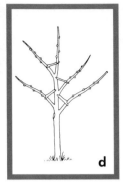

Fig. 3. TWO APPLE CULTIVARS, DELICIOUS AND GOLDEN DELICIOUS, WITH DIFFERENT GROWTH HABITS, AND THE SEQUENCE FOR PRUNING DELICIOUS: **a)** Growth habit of Golden Delicious; note the well-defined central leader, wide-angled crotches, and moderate extension growth; **b)** Growth habit of Delicious; note vigorous, upright growth competing with the central leader, excessive number of scaffold limbs, and narrow crotch angles; **c)** Delicious after scaffold selection and heading back the central-leader shoot; note spacing of scaffolds along the main trunk; **d)** Delicious after insertion of limb spreaders; spreading improves the crotch angle, reduces scaffold vigor, favors flower bud formation, reduces competition with the leader, and eliminates interference of lower scaffolds with the growth of scaffolds originating higher on the trunk.

central leader tree.

For vigorous, upright-growing cultivars such as Red Delicious, remove some of the lateral branches and spread the remaining branches to forty-five-degree angles, either by using wooden sticks as spacers or by hanging weights on the branches.

Try to position the scaffold limbs around the trunk with at least eight inches between the limbs along the trunk. It is important to position these limbs so they do not interfere with the development of other permanent limbs.

Stone Fruits

Stone fruit trees, including cherry, peach, nectarine, plum and prune, should be pruned in late spring. Peach and nectarine trees are highly susceptible to perennial canker, which is caused by a fungus that infects open wounds during cool temperatures. Delaying pruning until blossom time helps reduce the spread of this disease organism.

Cherry, plum or prune can be trained as a central leader tree as described for apple and pear, or trained with a modified leader, or trained into an open center (vase-shaped) tree.

Training a tree with a modified central leader is similar to training a central leader tree, except that after four or five good scaffold limbs have been selected on the leader, the top is removed.

After initial training, cherry, plum and prune trees need a few corrective cuts

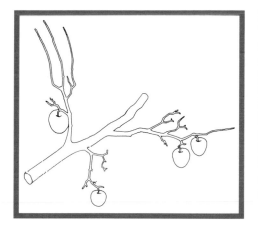

Fig. 4 ORIENTATION OF FRUITING BRANCHES: The upright branch is excessively vigorous, only moderately fruitful, and produces fruits that are often soft and poorly colored; the branch growing from the underside of a larger branch is heavily shaded and, as a result, is low in vigor and fruitfulness and produces small fruits of poor color; the horizontal branch is of moderate vigor and very fruitful, and because of good light exposure, produces fruit of superior color.

during the following five or six years, or until trees begin to bear fruit. During this time, limit pruning to the removal of watersprouts and limbs that cross and rub against a permanent branch.

Prune to prevent the development of bad crotches and weak unions that could split later under the weight of a crop. A bad crotch is a fork where two branches of equal diameter arise at a common point. Generally, one of these branches can be eliminated, but if it seems desirable to save both, cut one of them back severely;

it will then be smaller and develop as a lateral branch to the unpruned one.

Weak unions between the rootstock and the scion are common in some cultivars of fruit trees and most cultivars of sweet cherry. Often, vigorous shoots grow upright against the trunk or against other branches. To prevent this growth, choose limbs that spread out from the trunk at wide angles and remove those that grow upright against the trunk. Only an occasional cut is required, and pruning becomes gradually less necessary as

Fig. 5 PRUNING DROOPING BRANCHES:

Above, branches that droop downward are not well exposed to light and usually shade other branches.

Below, to prune, remove the ends of such branches back to a lateral in a near-horizontal position, and remove all branches growing downward from the bottom of larger branches.

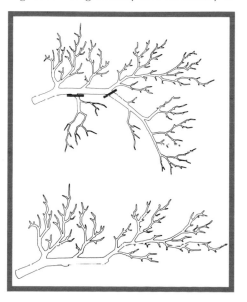

the tree comes into bearing.

Trees that have had proper corrective pruning from the beginning need little if any pruning during their early bearing years. Overpruning during the formative years delays bearing.

Peach trees, because of their growth habit, are not suitable as central leader or modified leader trees. Open center training, selecting only three scaffold limbs, is best for them. One-year-old nursery peach trees are usually three to six feet tall with some lateral branching. Laterals that were developed in the nursery as secondary shoots are generally too weak to make good framework branches. Prune these trees back to a height of 18 to 24 inches and cut off all laterals to encourage the growth of strong shoots on the trunk.

As soon as the shoots have grown a few inches, usually by the first of June, select three of the best shoots that are well positioned around the trunk, four to six inches apart, and remove all others. Equal growth and branching of these shoots results in an open center tree. Occasionally, nursery trees have one or two well-developed lateral branches in satisfactory positions and these can be used as scaffold limbs; then the main stem can be cut back to 30 inches and the laterals tipped off to uniform lengths.

Peach trees require extra attention following the first and second years' growth. The main scaffold branches should be lightly cut, or headed back, to outward-growing laterals. The purpose of heading back scaffolds is to continue the development of an open center tree that will be low, strong and spreading for convenient thinning, pest control, and harvesting. Leave the small shoots that cross in the center because they will bear the first fruits.

Pruning during the third and fourth years should be as light as possible, limited to removing only decidedly crowded limbs or low-hanging shaded branches in the center of the tree and heading back main scaffold limbs to laterals if they are too high or out of balance with others.

Pruning Bearing Apple and Pear Trees

Uniform vigor of the fruiting wood throughout a tree is ideal. Fruiting wood in the top of a tree, however, has the best exposure to sunlight, which is essential for plant and fruit growth, and is therefore more vigorous than the wood in the shaded lower portion of the tree. Also, orientation of fruiting wood along main lateral branches increases its vigor and fruiting potential.

For apples and pears, a cone-shaped tree intercepts light most efficiently. A cone shape is easy to maintain in a young tree, but is difficult to preserve as the tree ages. The top of a tree, which has the most vigorous growth, tends to spread and shade the lower limbs. When pruning, minimize small cuts, which have an invigorating effect. It is more effective to make one or two large cuts; either remove an entire branch or cut a major portion back to a vigorous fruiting lateral. Remove vigorous upright water sprouts and leave the weakest ones.

In the lower part of the tree, remove limbs that are shaded by other limbs. When limbs are young and fruitful, they are somewhat upright-angled or horizontal. As they become older, they droop and should be taken out. Also, eliminate all broken and crossing limbs.

Rejuvenating Old Apple or Pear Trees

Most old apple and pear trees are too tall for convenient pest control or harvesting. The top one-third of an old tree can be eliminated by making major cuts just above large side branches.

Subsequently, water sprouts will arise in the vicinity of these large cuts. These should be pruned or pulled during July and August while they are small, to prevent them from eventually shading the center of the tree. During dormant season, remove all strong upright shoots at points of origin. Water sprouts will form around these cuts, too. During the summer, prune or pull the strongest and leave a few weaker water sprouts to provide minimal shade and reduce sunscald.

Prune the lower part of old trees as previously described for bearing trees.

In the second or third season after severe pruning of old apple and pear trees, remove small limbs to create space between fruiting limbs.

Pruning Bearing Stone Fruit Trees

Cherry, plum and prune trees require the least pruning of all fruit trees. Generally they need no more than light heading back to strong lateral branches to keep trees in bounds; thinning out of branches to provide good light exposure for remaining limbs; and removal of dead, broken or diseased growth.

Peaches are borne on the previous season's growth. As trees attain full size, severe pruning renews fruiting wood. Terminal shoot growth of 12 to 18 inches is desirable. If shoot growth is weak or if lower limbs grow too long, cut branches back into two- or three-year-old wood; make cuts to an outward-growing side branch. After heading back all of the main branches, thin and space fruiting branches to six to eight inches apart. This spacing allows good light penetration to fruiting branches and allows development of new shoots for next year's crop.

Fruit Thinning

Fruit thinning, which is the removal of some developing fruits to improve size and quality of those left, is a form of pruning.

Thinning of fruit is seldom warranted

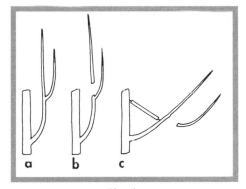

Fig.6.
Training an upright scaffold limb:
a) upright scaffold; note narrow crotch angle and smaller, upright lateral branch; **b)** incorrect procedure; thinning out to the upright does not improve the crotch angle and limb position or control vigorous vegetative growth; **c)** correct procedure; spreading the limb improves the crotch angle and properly positions the scaffold; remove the lateral, for it will be shaded by growth from the main scaffold limb.

on young trees. On mature fruit trees, early and proper thinning results in larger, better colored and higher quality fruit, and also promotes prolific blooming the following spring.

When fruits are clustered, remove all but one in each cluster. Remove small and/or unhealthy fruits first.

Leave potentially good fruits at the following spacings: peaches, four to eight inches apart (somewhat wider spacing for early cultivars); plums and prunes, four inches; apples, four to six inches.

The results are well worth the time invested in thinning. 🌿

PRUNING GRAPES & BRAMBLE & BUSH FRUITS

MARCIA EAMES-SHEAVLY

&

MARVIN P. PRITTS

Pruning and Training Grapes

YOUNG VINES

The four-arm Kniffen system (Figure 1) is recommended for training grapes in home gardens, although many other methods can be used. This system employs a trellis made by stringing two lines of galvanized wire (size 9, 10, or 11) or monofilament line between durable wood posts set about 24 feet apart. The top wire should be about six feet high and the lower (and parallel) wire about three feet high.

During the first year, when new shoots are about ten inches long, remove all but the strongest one and tie it to the bottom wire to hold it erect. Remove all other shoots and flower clusters as they arise, so that a single cane develops.

If the cane does not reach the top wire in the first year, treat the plant as a newly planted vine the following year.

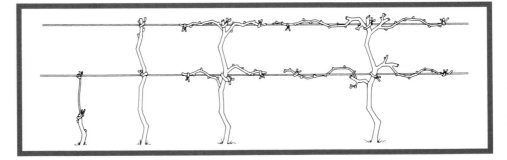

Fig.1. Stages of training a vine to the four-arm Kniffen system on a two-wire trellis.

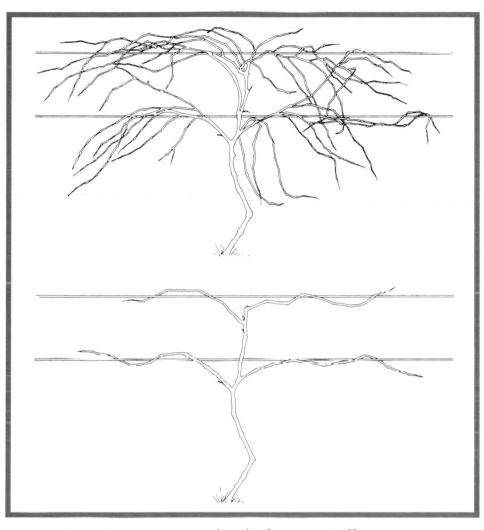

Fig.2. Grapevine trained to the four-arm Kniffen system:
above, unpruned; **below**, pruned.

In late winter or early spring, tie the two-year-old cane to the top trellis wire and cut it off just above the wire. Leave four to six buds in the vicinity of each wire and remove the rest. As new shoots begin to grow from the remaining buds, cut off any flower clusters that form.

In early spring of the third year, before new growth occurs, select a total of eight canes (four for each wire) and remove the rest. Tie one cane along each wire in each direction. Cut the remaining four canes, two at each wire, back to stubs containing two buds each.

MATURE VINES

In early spring, remove the fruiting canes from the previous year. Tie one of the canes from each stub (left last year) to a

31

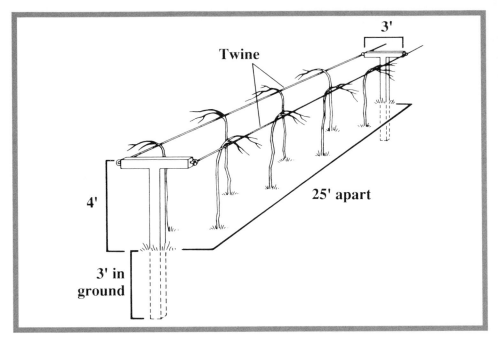

Fig.3. Temporary trellis for primocane fruiting raspberry plants.

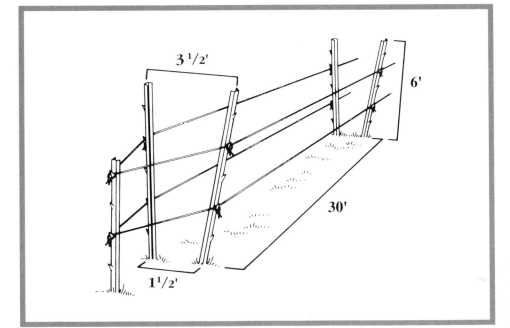

Fig.4. A V-trellis system for raspberry plants.

trellis wire, one in each direction on each wire, and cut each cane to leave ten buds. These are the fruiting arms for the new season.

Cut the remaining four canes from last year's stubs back to two buds, thus forming new stubs.

In subsequent years, adjust the number of buds left on each arm. Too many buds result in lower fruit quality; insufficient buds reduce yield.

NEGLECTED VINES

To renew old neglected grape vines, prune in stages. The first year, cut away old arms, and allow a few new canes to develop from near the base of the old trunk.

The next year, select one vigorous cane arising from near the base, and tie it to the trellis wires to form a new trunk. Treat this sprout as a newly planted vine, and cut off the old trunk after another season or two.

Pruning Bramble Fruits

TRELLISING

Several systems of trellising are employed by some growers of bramble fruits. Many growers of primocane-fruiting raspberries (main branch fruits first year) employ a temporary trellis during the fall harvest season. One temporary system that works well consists of T-shaped metal or wooden posts with three-foot crossarms with screw eyes at the ends. Baling twine attached to the crossarms is cheap, yet strong enough to hold canes erect temporarily. (See Figure 3).

A permanent trellis of the "V" type improves production of floricane fruiting raspberries (main branch fruits second year). Opposing posts are set into the ground at 20 to 30 degree angles. (See Figure 4.)

Fruiting canes are tied to the wires on the outside of the V in early spring, and new canes (primocanes) are permitted to grow on the inside of the V. Spraying, pruning and harvesting are made easier because floricanes are accessible and pri-

mocane interference is minimal. Yields often are increased because the amount of light reaching the foliage canopy is increased.

Vigorous plants, such as blackberry, are often tied to a trellis similar to that used for grapes, with one wire at three feet, the other at six.

Primocane Fruiting Raspberries

This type of raspberry plant produces fruit at the top of first-year canes in late summer and on the lower portion of the same canes in early summer of the second year. Most growers choose to sacrifice the early summer crop in favor of the superior quality of the late summer crop.

For the late season crop, cut primocane fruiting raspberry plants as close to the ground as possible each spring, so buds will break from below soil surface.

Floricane Fruiting Raspberries and Blackberries

Floricane fruiting types produce fruit on second-year canes. During the flowering and fruiting of the second-year canes, first-year canes are growing.

After fruiting, two-year old canes are cut to the ground. Early the next spring, one-year-old canes are topped at a desired height and thinned to a desired number, depending on type of berry.

Some growers prefer to simply mow half of a bramble planting each year during the dormant season. This is a low-labor system, but quality, size and total yield of the berries is reduced.

A third method is to remove all but four or five new canes per linear foot of row each year in June, when they are about eight inches tall. Red raspberries are best pruned in mid-March in colder climates. Remove winter-killed tips. Thin out canes to leave three or four per linear foot of row. Remove two-year-old canes at ground level after fruiting. (See Figure 5.)

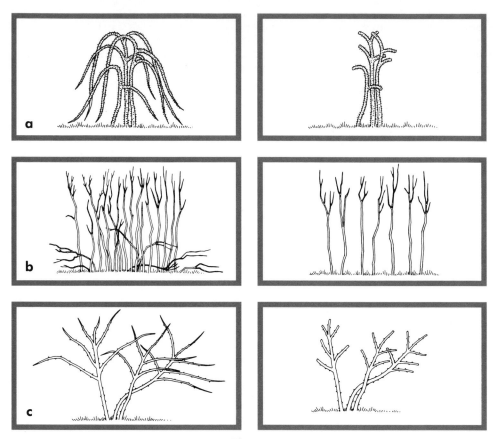

Fig.5.
RASPBERRY PLANTS, BEFORE AND AFTER PRUNING:
a) black; **b)** red; **c)** purple

Black raspberries should have new canes summer pruned (June in north temperate states) to about 24 inches. Thin out to two or three canes per foot of row. Remove two-year canes after fruiting. In March, remove winter-killed tips.

For purple raspberries, prune canes as high as trellis permits; remove tips that are winter-killed. Thin to three or four canes per linear foot of row. Remove fruiting canes in fall or early spring.

Thorny blackberries should be pruned in summer to three or four feet high. In early spring, remove old canes, thin out one-year-old canes to two per linear foot and shorten lateral branches to 12 to 16 inches.

Thornless blackberries are best thinned in summer to six canes per foot. Remove fruiting canes after fruiting. In spring, shorten canes to the upper trellis wire, or wind them around the wire and shorten laterals to about 18 inches.

Pruning Blueberries

During the first year after planting blueberry bushes, remove all flowers as they appear to divert energy into vegetative growth.

Fig.6.
BLUEBERRY PLANTS, BEFORE AND AFTER PRUNING:
left, unpruned; **right,** pruned yearly.

Each succesive year, prune in early spring. Remove any winter-killed wood. Topping canes to stimulate lateral growth generally is not recommended.

The ideal blueberry bush should have no more than sixteen canes, ranging from small new ones to older canes no more than one inch in diameter. This can be achieved by allowing only two new canes to grow each year after planting until the bush is eight years old. Then the oldest canes should be one inch in diameter. Since canes one-half to one inch in diameter produce more fruit than larger canes, remove old canes at ground level when they exceed one inch in diameter.

As years go by, a blueberry bush pruned in this way behaves as an efficient young plant even though the root portion is old.

Pruning Currants and Gooseberries

Prune currants and gooseberries when plants are dormant, in late winter or early spring. Remove any branches that lie along the ground as well as those that are broken, diseased and/or insect-infested (e.g. San Jose scale).

After the first year of growth, remove all but six to eight of the most vigorous stems. At the end of the second growing season, leave several one-year-old shoots and several two-year-old canes.

By the end of the third year, approximately four canes for each season should remain, twelve in all.

In the fourth year, remove the oldest canes and allow four or so sturdy one-year-old stems to develop. Continue to remove four-year-old stems each spring.

Pruning Elderberries

Elderberry bushes send up many new shoots each year. These branch and fruit during their second season. Fruiting is reduced on three-year-old stems, and is poor on four-year-old stems. Thus, each year in late winter or early spring, remove all four-year-old stems and any weak and spindly one-year shoots. ✿

PRUNING DECIDUOUS & NEEDLED EVERGREEN SHRUBS

EDWIN D. CARPENTER

Pruning is an important element of the proper care of deciduous and needled evergreen shrubs — as essential as watering, fertilizing, mulching and pest control. Some yearly pruning is necessary for almost all deciduous and evergreen shrubs, for example, to control growth so the plants will not outgrow their allotted spaces. Yet pruning is often misunderstood and neglected.

Formal Versus Natural

For many years terms like "gum drops" and "lolly-pops" have been used to describe the shape of formally sheared shrubs. Some people like this formal style of pruning; some do not.

There are times, however, when sheared, formal designs are appropriate. Espaliers, topiaries and pollarded trees, for example, can add a touch of formal

DR. EDWIN D. CARPENTER *is Professor of Ornamental Horticulture and Cooperative Extension Specialist in Ornamental Horticulture/Merchandising at the University of Connecticut, and an active member of Garden Writers of America.*

elegance to landscapes.

For the most part, modern landscaping in the United States calls for informal, or natural-form, pruning. Plants should not be sheared into tight geometrical figures. They should be pruned according to their natural shapes; in most cases, it should not even be apparent that pruning was done.

Figure 1 illustrates the difference between formal and informal pruning. *Figure 3* illustrates informal pruning for spreading needled evergreens and for upright needled evergreens.

Pruning Methods

Two basic methods of pruning are shown in *Figure 4*. Thinning and heading back work together to keep plants in bounds. Thinning opens up the plant, and heading back controls height and spread.

Thinning out is a process of removing a branch at its point of origin at a branch union (a "Y"), or at a lateral bud, or at ground level. Old, tall stems are removed first, making room for new side branch-

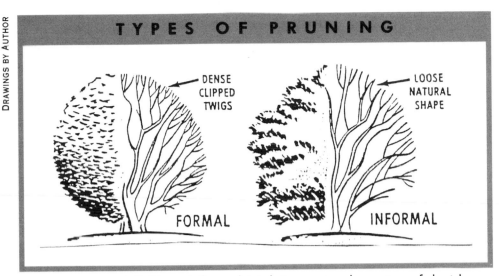

TYPES OF PRUNING

DENSE CLIPPED TWIGS

LOOSE NATURAL SHAPE

FORMAL

INFORMAL

Figure 1: Formal (left) vs. informal (right) or natural pruning of deciduous and needled evergreen shrubs.

es. This kind of pruning results in a more open plant, without stimulating excessive new growth or changing the natural form of the plant.

There are two types of thinning: renewal and rejuvenation. Renewal pruning should be done on deciduous shrubs that are old and neglected. Shrubs are "renewed" by removing (cutting to the ground or nearly so) one-third of the old stems the first year, and removing the remaining two-thirds of old stems over the next two years.

Rejuvenation is more drastic: All the branches of an old shrub are removed at once by cutting to ground level or slightly above. This draconian procedure should be done only on shrubs known to respond well to it (some are listed in **Table 3**). The best time for rejuvenation pruning is late winter or early spring before new growth starts.

Heading back, the second basic method of pruning deciduous shrubs, is the removal of only terminal portions of branches (**Figure 4**). This procedure

reduces overall height and width of a plant. As a result, heading back stimulates new growth lower on the cut stems, making the plant more dense.

Too much heading back in a single season will generally cause more growth to occur than was pruned off. To be effective, heading back should remove only a small percentage of top growth in one season.

Pruning to enhance the natural growth habit of needled evergreen shrubs involves keeping them open for good light penetration and keeping them in bounds. The thinning method described above for deciduous shrubs is recommended for needled evergreens as well.

There are times when heading back is also needed (see **Figure 5**). Heading back cuts, like thinning cuts, should be made at a branch union or just above a bud.

Figure 5A illustrates pruning cuts needed to maintain a natural, compact, upright growth form.

Figure 5B illustrates pruning back to a bud or branch union to control the spread of a plant.

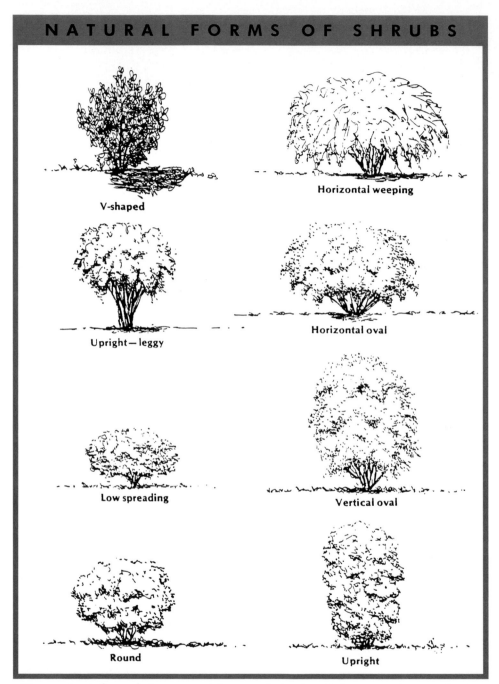

V-shaped

Horizontal weeping

Upright — leggy

Horizontal oval

Low spreading

Vertical oval

Round

Upright

Figure 2: A few of the natural forms of shrubs. Before pruning study the plant and its form. Decide what you wish to accomplish before pruning.

Dwarf pine showing candles of new growth.

Figure 5C shows the removal of an overly long central leader.

Figure 5D illustrates the removal of multiple leaders. One leader is preferred for a stronger plant. Remove the weakest, leaving the best one to become the central leader.

All needled evergreens can be pruned as noted above, except pines. Pines put out a single flush of growth per year and stop. To avoid dead stubs and poor appearance, pines must be pruned in the "candle stage" of growth (see Figure 6).

To promote dense growth, prune the candles when they are two to three inches long, when the new stem is still soft. This new growth can be shortened by as much as three-fourths of its length with pruning shears or a sharp knife. Often it

Figure 3: Two natural forms of needled evergreen shrubs. Spreading types are represented by junipers and yews, arborvitae and falsecypress.

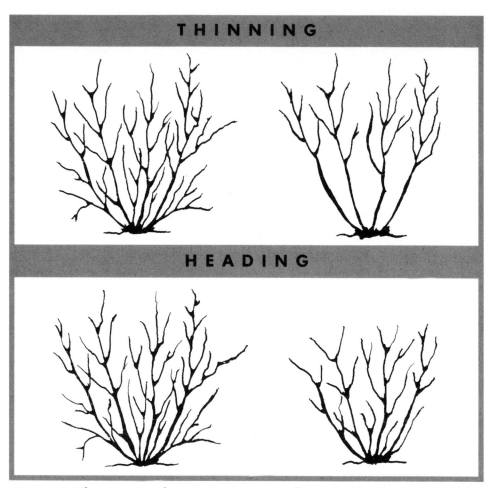

Figure 4: Thinning involves removing entire branches back to where they began. Heading, shortens branches, rather than removing them entirely.

can be snapped off readily with one's fingers. Do not remove last year's growth.

When to Prune

According to the old adage, pruning can be done anytime the knife is sharp. This simply means that broken, damaged, insect-ridden and/or disease-infested stems can be removed whenever you see them. Other light pruning can be done anytime with little effect on the plant.

But moderate to heavy pruning can be a problem if done at the wrong time. Since landscape plants are often grown for flowers and/or fruits, it is important to know when plants produce flower buds. Tables 1 and 2 illustrate how to prune according to when flower buds are formed.

With the exception of pines, needled evergreen shrubs can be pruned most anytime, except late summer. Needled and deciduous shrubs shouldn't be pruned at this time (August through mid-September in northern climates) because it may encourage

Figure 5A: Pruning an upright or spreading needled evergreen for compact growth.

Figure 5C: Pruning to shorten a leader that has grown too long.

Figure 5B: Pruning a needled evergreen to control growth in spread.

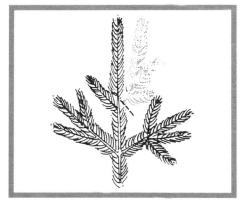

Figure 5D: Pruning to remove all but one leader when multiple leaders form. Leave the best of the leaders that grow.

41

TABLE 1	Spring flowering shrubs should be pruned immediately after flowering. Flower buds develop during the previous summer's growth. If pruned before flowering in the spring, flower buds will be removed and no flowers or fruits will be available during the current season.

SCIENTIFIC NAME	COMMON NAME
Amelanchier species	Shadblow
Berberis species	Barberry
Calycanthus species	Sweetshrub
Cercis species	Redbud
Chaenomeles species	Flowering quince
Cornus florida	Flowering dogwood
Cornus kousa	Kousa dogwood
Cornus mas	Cornelian cherry
Deutzia species	Deutzia
Forsythia species	Forsythia
Kolkwitzia amabilis	Beautybush
Ligustrum species	Privet
Lonicera species	Honeysuckle
Magnolia species	Magnolia
Malus species	Crabapple
Philadelphus species	Mock orange
Prunus species	Flowering cherry and plum
Rhododendron species	Rhododendron and azaleas
Rhodotypos scandens	Black jetbead
Rosa species	Climbers and shrub roses
Spiraea thunbergii	Thunberg spirea
Spiraea x *vanhouttei*	Vanhoute spirea
Styrax japonica	Japanese snowball
Syringa species	Common, Chinese and French lilacs
Viburnum x *burkwoodii*	Burkwood viburnum
Viburnum carlesii	Korean spice viburnum
Viburnum lantana	Wayfaring tree
Viburnum opulus	European cranberrybush
Viburnum plicatum tomentosum	Doublefile viburnum

new growth which won't have time to harden off and may be killed by frost. The time to prune pines is when candles of new growth are two to three inches long. In Connecticut, this normally occurs during the first two weeks of June.

Finally, a word of caution. The pruning recommendations here are offered as guidelines. For species not mentioned, and for local conditions that influence pruning techniques and timing, consult local authorities or one of the number of reference books that are available. 🌰

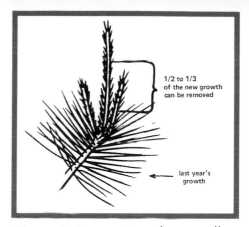

1/2 to 1/3 of the new growth can be removed

last year's growth

Figure 6: Prune pine when candles are two to three inches long.

TABLE 2	Summer flowering shrubs should be pruned before spring vegetative growth begins. These plants develop flower buds after stem growth has started. Pruning from late November to early spring before buds break is recommended.

SCIENTIFIC NAME	COMMON NAME
Acanthopanax species	Aralia
Buddleia species	Butterflybush
Callicarpa species	Beautybush
Clematis species	Clematis
Hibiscus syriacus	Shrub althea
Hydrangea paniculata 'Grandiflora'	P.G. hydrangea
Hydrangea quercifolia	Oakleaf hydrangea
Rosa species	Hybrid tea rose

TABLE 3	A short list of plants which can be rejuvenated by cutting back to the ground. They generally will return to usefulness in short periods of time. Spring flowering plants may not flower for two or three years when rejuvenated in early spring.

SCIENTIFIC NAME	COMMON NAME
Buddleia davidii	Orange-eye butterflybush
Clematis x jackmanii	Jackman clematis
Forsythia species	Forsythia
Hibiscus syriacus	Shrub althea
Hydrangea arborescens 'Grandiflora'	Hills-of-snow
Hydrangea quercifolia	Oakleaf hydrangea
Lonicera species	Honeysuckle
Polygonum aubertii	Silver fleece vine
Spiraea species	Spirea
Syringa species	Lilac

PRUNING BROADLEAF EVERGREENS

FRED C. GALLE

The basic principles for pruning broadleaf evergreens are the same as for deciduous shrubs (see page 36). As a rule, to avoid a prolonged sheared look, prune in early spring just before new growth starts. Except for hedges and for special effects, prune to the natural shape and growth habit of the plant. Most of the broadleaf evergreens can receive corrective pruning and light pinching to increase branching at any season of the year.

Old, leggy, multiple-stemmed plants, such as privets, hollies and camellias, can be sculpture-pruned into beautifully formed, large shrubs or small trees by removing lower branches. Thinning out the crown and removal of suckers or feather growth will also increase the attractiveness of old plants (see Pruning for Character and Size Control, page 56).

FRED C. GALLE *is former Director of Horticulture of Callaway Gardens, Pine Mountain, Georgia, and former Vice President of the Ida Cason Callaway Foundation. He has authored two books on azaleas and is working on a holly volume. Fred has been active in many horticultural organizations. His awards and honors include the Liberty Hyde Bailey Medal of the American Horticultural Society, the Gold Medal of the American Rhododendron Society and the Arthur Hoyt Scott Garden Award from Swarthmore College.*

If complete rejuvenation is required, it should be done in late winter or early spring by cutting the plants to six to eighteen inches from the ground. The strong vegetative growth that subsequently develops in the spring will require thinning and pinching to form compact plants.

An alternative to complete rejuvenation, called "coat rack" pruning, may be used with spindly open specimens of American holly (*Ilex opaca*), English holly (*I. aquifolium*), horned (Chinese) holly (*I. cornuta*) and others. Branches are severely cut back, but the general form of the plant is retained. Such a plant will look stiff (like a coat rack), but new growth will quickly fill in to form a thickly branched plant.

Holly and Osmanthus

Hollies, depending upon species and cultivars, vary from densely conical or rounded to open and multiple-branched. Observe the natural shape and prune to enhance the habit of growth. Pruning of fruiting branches at Christmastime provides material for holiday decorations. Keep in mind, however, that some hollies produce fruit on old wood; you will be removing flower buds that were produced in late summer. Hollies in this group include lusterleaf holly (*Ilex latifolia*), horned holly (*I. cornuta*) and its many cultivars such as 'Burfordii'. Heavy pruning of these in winter will reduce the abundance of fruit the next season.

In contrast, most hollies produce fruits on the current season's growth. In this group are several hollies indigenous to the United States and their cultivars: American holly (*I. opaca*), Topal holly (*I. x attenuata*), cassine (dahoon) holly (*I. cassine*) and myrtleleaf holly (*I. myrtifolia*). Yaupon holly (*I. vomitoria*) is the only U.S. indigenous holly that produces flowers and fruits on old wood.

Some introduced holly species also bear fruits on new growth: long-stalk holly (*I. pedunculosa*) and Chinese holly (*I. purpurea* [*chinensis*]).

Moderate pruning of fruited branches of the above "new growth fruiters" will not affect fruit production for the next season. Japanese holly (*I. crenata*) and inkberry (*I. glabra*), both of which have relatively inconspicuous black fruits, should be pruned in early spring before new growth starts and touched up once or twice during the growing season as needed, especially if used as hedges.

Osmanthus species of foreign origin, such as *O. fragrans*, *O. heterophyllus*, *O. x fortunei*, *O. armatus* and *O. delavayi*, are prized for their attractive foliage and their fragrant creamy-white flowers in late fall and winter. Cutting of small flowering branches allows one to enjoy the delightful fragrance indoors. Heavy pruning, if needed, should be delayed until early spring.

Osmanthus americanus (devilweed), a native to the United States, flowers in the spring on old wood and bears fruit in the fall. Thus, early-spring pruning reduces flowering and fruiting, but pruning after flowering reduces fruiting. Take your pick!

Camellia and Pyracantha

Prune camellias in late winter and early spring after flowering. Summer pruning of leggy growth is often required to keep plants compact. Old leggy plants can be sculpture-pruned to a treelike form or rejuvenated completely by cutting off all branches 6 to 12 inches from the ground. This is a drastic treatment and not all may respond to this heavy pruning. For these special old-timers it is best to extend the rejuvenation over a three-year period by removing a third of the branches each year.

The new vigorous growth from cut-back plants will require thinning out some of the excessive growth and also pinching of the new shoots to develop lateral growth.

Disbudding of flower buds from some *Camellia japonica* cultivars is often required to produce better flowers. Some cultivars develop a considerable number of large, rounded flower buds that should be thinned out to produce perfect specimen blossoms. Care should be taken in removing the large flower buds to avoid disturbance of the long, slender leaf buds. *Camellia sasanqua* and *C. reticulata* plants seldom need to be disbudded. Old blossoms and swollen fungus-diseased leaves should be removed and destroyed.

The blossoms and fruit of pyracantha (firethorn) are produced on short spur-like branches from two-year-old wood. Thus, heavy pruning in any one year will reduce the colorful berry crop that fall. Spring and summer pruning of new growth will aid in keeping vigorous plants in bounds. For confined areas, use the less vigorous dwarf varieties. Diseased brown leaves and branches resulting from fire blight should be removed by cutting back into fresh, disease-free stems.

Ericaceous Plants

Mountain-laurel (*Kalmia latifolia*) and pieris (*Pieris japonica* and *P. floribunda*) produce flower buds on old wood and should be pruned after flowering. Old, overgrown specimens of these species can be renovated by severe pruning in

A big American holly before severe pruning (hatracking).

The same plant after "hatracking."

The same plant two years after "hatracking."

late winter or early spring. Both heath and heather (*Erica* and *Calluna*) are best pruned by removing flowers as they fade. Ragged or out-of-bounds old plants can be cut back in spring or summer.

Rhododendrons that appear thin and leggy can be thickened by pruning off the terminal rosette of leaves to just above a lower rosette of leaves, not leaving a long stub. New vegetative shoots will develop from the dormant buds in the axil of each leaf of the rosette.

Disbudding, the removal of leafy growth buds with thumb and forefinger, is an easy way to develop compactness on young plants, but time-consuming on large ones. Once the terminal leaf bud is removed, dormant sidebuds will develop at the end of the branch. Flower buds are larger and more rotund than the tapered, slender leaf buds.

Deheading of rhododendrons is the removal of old flower trusses before they develop seed capsules. Failure to do this often results in the rhododendron producing a good display of flowers only in alternate years. This does not apply to azaleas or small-leaved rhododendrons.

Others

Boxwoods are most attractive with their dense, billowy habit. Light pruning and pinching of new growth will increase branching.

The beautiful evergreen daphnes generally require little pruning except cutting of the largest stems of fragrant early spring flowers to use in the home.

Mahonias and nandinas often get leggy and bare at the bottom as they mature. An annual removal of a third of the old canes at ground level in early spring will allow new leafy shoots to develop, forming fine specimens after three years. When not many canes are present, a complete rejuvenation can be obtained by cutting off all the leggy canes at one time.

PRUNING DISEASED PLANTS

When pruning trees and shrubs that have wilt, canker, fireblight, gall or other diseases that affect some but not all parts of a plant, care must be taken to avoid spreading the disease to healthy tissue.

Don't prune when plants — diseased or robust — are wet. Water is an effective vehicle for nasty little organisms.

Always cut well below diseased areas, as much as six inches, into healthy tissue.

At this point, some pruning texts add: and sterilize pruning tools after every cut. Alcohol, the isopropyl kind, has been recommended for sterilizing tools between cuts, or at least between plants. Household bleach is sometimes mentioned, but it may be corrosive to some metal surfaces.

Some authorities claim that such quick dip (on pruning saws, more likely quick wipe) treatments are ineffective. Indeed, few surgeons rely on such a "sterilization" of scalpels between patients.

One pruning authority, when questioned recently about sterilizing pruning tools, replied, "Nobody is doing it."

Well, at least pay attention to the second and third paragraphs above.

And burn, discard or bury the diseased prunings in accordance with local laws and regulations.

47

PRUNING CONIFEROUS EVERGREEN TREES

FREEK VRUGTMAN

A tree looks best when it attains its natural size and shape. Prune coniferous trees only for a definite reason, never just for the sake of pruning. Before you prune try to visualize what will happen if you do prune.

Broken Leaders

Should a leader be broken, a lateral branch can be trained to become a new leader. The best time to do this is spring when the branches are more flexible and can be bent carefully without breaking. A

FREEK VRUGTMAN *is Curator of Collections, Royal Botanic Gardens, Hamilton, Ontario, Canada.*

brace or splint (Fig. 1) is used to hold the new leader in place throughout the following growing season, after which the brace should be removed. Strips of a nylon stocking or fabric used in figure-eight fashion make good ties and are to be preferred to twine or wire, which may injure the young bark.

Two Types of Coniferous Trees

Firs, Douglas-firs, pines, spruces and a few less common conifers produce their branches in whorls around the main axis. Given good soil, enough space, light and water, these trees will normally grow into symmetrical conical specimens requiring

Figure 1

Figure 2

Figure 3

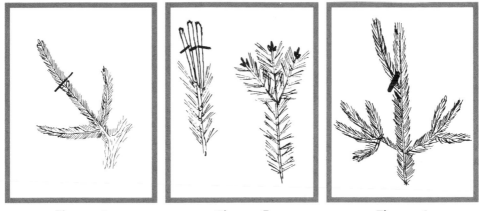

Figure 4   Figure 5   Figure 6

little pruning. It may happen that a tree is very vigorous and the annual growth of the leader is long, so long, in fact, that the whorls of lateral shoots are quite far apart, with conspicuous bare spaces between the upper whorls. These open spaces can be reduced by pruning the growing leader to about half its size in the spring during the active growing season (Fig. 2). Do not cut before the new growth is well underway, and do not prune after the new growth is nearly mature, because no new terminal bud can be formed from hardened tissue.

Lateral growth can be checked in a similar way, or you can remove the terminal bud of a side branch (Fig. 3). If even greater size control is needed, cut the branches back to an inner bud (Fig. 4). More drastic pruning than this is ill advised, as these plants are incapable of regenerating from older wood. Pines may be pruned in the "candle stage" when new young shoots, with their immature needles packed tightly around the stem, look like candles (Fig. 5). When nipped in half at this stage, the annual growth is reduced and buds will be formed at the end of the pruned shoot. Sometimes secondary or even tertiary leaders develop; these should be removed as soon as possible and not left to develop for another

Figure 7

growing season (Fig. 6).

Arbovitae, cedars, cypresses, false-cypresses, giant sequoia, hemlocks, junipers, redwood and yews are characterized by a less regular pattern with buds and branches not arranged in whorls. Slowing down the growth by pruning can be done more easily than in conifers with a whorled growth pattern. Lateral branches that are too long can be

49

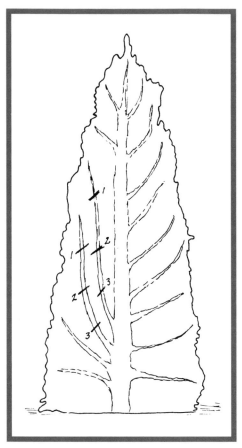

Figure 8

Figure 9

Figure 10

pruned back to within the periphery of the foliage where the cutting point will be hidden, provided the branches still carry sufficient foliage to continue to grow (Fig. 7). Only giant sequoia and yews should be pruned back more severely, even right back to the trunk if necessary; latent buds will break and give rise to a new crown in a few years.

Single trunks also are to be preferred for coniferous trees in this group, but occasionally lateral branches develop into secondary leaders and remain undetected for years. This happens most frequently in arbovitae, false-cypresses and junipers. Visually this is no disaster since the plant as a whole retains its characteristic shape; structurally, however, such a plant is at a disadvantage, particularly in regions where snow storms and ice storms are frequent and where multistemmed conifers are the first ones to suffer damage. Secondary leaders may be

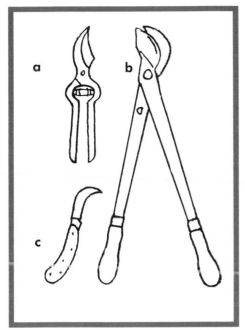

Figure 11
a) Pruning shears;
b) Lopping shears;
c) Pruning knife

pruned back gradually over a period of several years until only a side branch remains and the gap has been filled in gradually by lateral growth of the surrounding branches (Fig. 8)

Pruning to Correct Problems

Sometimes a Colorado blue spruce or other evergreen trees will grow in an extremely lopsided manner, even without being crowded by other plants or without exposure to prevailing winds (Fig. 9). Chances are, the plant is a grafted one and the scion used in grafting came from a lateral shoot. Such a plant needs to be staked until it gains the desired posture. If one side of the plant produces more vigorous growth than the opposite side, it will require some careful pruning (removal of

buds, pruning during spring growth or pruning to an inner bud as discussed earlier) to obtain a symmetrical tree.

You may be tempted to remove the lower branches of large evergreens if they interfere with mowing the lawn, but keep in mind that, once removed, there will be a gap that cannot be filled again by your tree (Fig. 10). Make sure the plant continues to receive full exposure to light. Do not wait until the lower branches begin to turn brown; once the needles have turned brown there is no chance for recovery. Do not expect three trees to grow to maturity gracefully where there is only space for one.

Tools and Techniques

For all pruning work, use the proper tools such as hand pruning shears (secateurs), lopping shears, a pruning saw and a pruning knife (Fig. 11). Be sure the tools are sharp and free of rust; they will be easier to work with and do a better job. Always make clean, smooth cuts without ragged edges. If you use a saw, smooth the surface of the cut with the pruning knife. Do not leave any stubs; they will die back. Do not damage buds, cut just beyond (above or outside) a bud (Fig. 12). If you detect or suspect disease, clean tools after each cut.

If, after the pruning is done, you stand back and can hardly detect where the tree was pruned, you are looking at a job well done. 🌲

Figure 12

PRUNING AT TRANSPLANTING

ELTON M. SMITH

The objective of transplanting is to establish the plant in its new site as quickly as possible. Proper pruning at this time helps a woody plant survive the disruption and injuries caused by its removal from the nursery or site where it was grown. The original source of the plant may have a significant bearing on the need for pruning landscape plants at the time of transplanting.

Nursery Grown vs. Collected Stock

Most landscape plants are produced in commercial nurseries where regular pruning is part of the cultural program. Thus it's unusual to need more than minimal pruning at transplanting time.

Plants grown in a nursery are often transplanted and/or root-pruned during various stages of production, which also helps promote a compact root system. Nursery-raised plants have a much higher success rate than those collected from the wild.

Some landscape plants offered for sale, however, are collected from native stands and will need more pruning for successful transplanting. The shape of collected plants is usually not up to the standard of nursery-grown plants. Pruning will be important to shape the plant (especially if

DR. ELTON M. SMITH *is Professsor of Horticulture with Cooperative Extension Service, The Ohio State University. He is active in a number of professional organizations, and for years has orchestrated the Ohio Nursery Short Course in Columbus, Ohio.*

it is a tree), to remove dead or pest-infested portions, if any, and (most important) to reduce top growth to compensate for a significant loss of root growth.

Some states have plant labeling laws requiring labels which indicate if plants offered for sale have been collected from the wild. If the quality of plants in a sales lot is questionable, be certain to inquire.

Sometimes plants may be moved from one site in the landscape to another, and the amount of pruning necessary will vary depending upon size, shape, species, health and other factors.

Woody Plants from the Garden Center

Nursery-grown stock in the garden center is available in several forms. Some forms will need more extensive pruning than others.

Balled and Burlapped

Trees larger than two inches in diameter are sold balled and burlapped (B&B), as are most field-grown evergreens and larger field-grown shrubs. Limited — if any — pruning is required and no root pruning is possible.

In some sections of the U.S., some trees and other plants are produced in fabric containers inserted at planting into the ground. These plants require a minimum of pruning of either the top growth or root system when transplanted.

Bare Root

Many deciduous plants are sold in early spring in bare root form. These plants are usually lower in price, require some root and top pruning and have a lower transplant survival rate. Deciduous shrubs, as well as trees less than two inches in diameter, are often sold bare root.

Container-Grown

Very little if any pruning is necessary with above-ground portions of container-grown plants. However, survival may be enhanced if the lower half of the root system is cut vertically and spread out horizontally when planted.

Roots of container-grown plants grow much deeper than similar plants in the field because container media have excellent drainage and aeration, and roots usually grow to the bottom of the container. Planting these bottom roots at the base of a planting hole in heavy soil may result in planting too deep, and a lack of air at this depth will lead to the death of those roots.

To increase chances of survival, according to research in Maryland, cut the root system vertically with a spade from the base to approximately half way towards the main stem. Then spread the cut portions horizontally in the planting hole to position them nearer the surface, where soil conditions are more favorable for root growth. Splitting the root system stops the circular habit of growth that the roots developed from growing in the containers and forces roots to develop new lateral roots into the backfill.

Splitting the rootball of container-grown shrubs is especially important if roots have become pot-bound in the container, and/or if the soil at the planting site is clayey and poorly drained.

Field-Potted

An increasing number of plants, especially narrowleaf evergreens such as yews and junipers, are field-potted. They are grown in a nursery field to salable size, then dug and potted prior to sale.

These should not be treated as container-grown plants. Typically, they can be identified in the retail lot because they are in a fiber-composition pot rather than a plastic container. Most growers dig these in autumn and overwinter them prior to delivery for spring sale. New root activity often occurs during this period, increasing the chances of survival after transplanting. Transplant survival rates are usually quite high for these plants, although not as high as for container-grown plants. Vertical cutting of the root system is not recommended for field-potted plants.

Packaged

Packaged plants are commonly available in garden outlets during the spring season. These are plants which have been dug bare root and the roots packed in an organic medium such as peat moss or a bark mix and wrapped in plastic. Only a minimum of pruning is required at transplanting because most of these plants have been graded and pruned prior to processing.

Pruning by Plant Group

The amount of pruning required at transplanting also varies according to plant group.

Deciduous Trees

The first pruning after trees are obtained consists of removing broken, crowded, crossing and pest-infested branches. Branches that were cracked at the base or otherwise injured when bundled and packed should be removed or shortened.

As a rule, the central leader of a tree should not be pruned. A couple of exceptions to this rule are naturally low-branched trees or when multiple-stemmed plants are desired. Trees with a central leader, such as linden, sweet gum or pin oak, may need little or no pruning except to eliminate branches competing with the central leader; these should be removed or shortened. Some pruning may be necessary to maintain desired shape — shortening extra-vigorous shoots, for example.

The height of the lowest branch can be from a few inches from the ground for screening or windbreaks, to seven to twelve feet or more above the ground for shade trees and for trees near streets, decks, patios, etc. "Limbing-up" (removal of lower branches) is usually conducted over a period of years after transplanting until the desired height of lowest branches is reached.

When planting container-grown plants in heavy soils, split the lower half of the root system and spread the roots horizontally. This practice will prune the roots, thus encouraging new laterals, prevent girdling roots and raise the lower roots closer to the soil surface.

For greatest strength, branches selected as permanent "scaffold" branches must have wide angles of attachment with the trunk. Branch angles less than 30 degrees from the main trunk are prone to breakage, while those between 60 degrees and 90 degrees have a very small breakage rate, according to research in California.

Vertical branch spacing and radial branch distribution are important. If this has been neglected in the nursery it can at least be begun at transplanting.

Major scaffold branches of shade trees should be spaced at least twelve inches and preferably twenty to twenty-four inches apart. Closely spaced branches become long and thin, with few lateral branches and poor structural strength.

Radial branch distribution should allow five to seven scaffold branches to fill the circle of space around a trunk. Radial spacing prevents one limb from overshadowing another, which in turn reduces competition for light and nutrients. Remove or prune shoots that are too low, too close or too vigorous in relation to the leader and branches selected to become the scaffold branches.

The rule of pruning away one-third of the top growth at transplanting to compensate for root loss should not be necessary for properly pruned nursery-grown plants.

Too much pruning at transplanting, according to research in Oklahoma, reduces plant size and does not improve chances of survival.

However, if little pruning was done at the nursery or the plants were collected, considerable pruning may be necessary to achieve a central leader, the desired shape and proper branch spacing and radial distribution.

Trees that should be pruned and are not pruned at transplanting time will prune themselves by dying back in time. Corrective pruning at transplanting will reduce or eliminate branch and twig dieback, assum-

Left: fabric container. Right: bare root. Plants harvested bare root will require more pruning.

Trees can be successfully produced in containers and survival is usually high with a minimum of pruning.

ing other conditions are optimal.

When transplanting a bare root tree, the only root pruning that should be needed is removal of broken or damaged roots. Do not cut roots to fit them into a planting hole that is too small, but rather increase the diameter of the hole to accommodate the roots without bending or crowding them.

Deciduous Shrubs

When shrubs are transplanted bare root, some pruning may be necessary. Light pruning of roots may be needed if any are broken, damaged or dead. Branches should be pruned by the thinning method — not shearing — to reduce the overall plant size by one-half or more. Research at Ohio State University indicates that survival and regrowth of deciduous shrubs was increased with removal of one-half or more of the branches of bare root plants at planting time.

Shrubs transplanted with a ball of soil or from a container require little, if any, pruning. Occasionally, branches are damaged in transit and these should be removed. Prune only to maintain desired size and shape.

Container-grown shrubs with pot-bound roots, and/or those which will be planted in heavy soil, benefit from splitting of the root mass as described above

in the section "Container-Grown."

Evergreens

Most evergreens are sold B&B or in a container and, as with deciduous shrubs, little pruning of branches is necessary.

The root-splitting technique, descibed above under "Container-Grown," is usually beneficial to evergreens at transplanting time, especially if roots are pot bound and/or the soil is heavy.

Root Pruning Research

Research conducted in Minnesota indicates that the following metal compounds have been found to be effective root pruning agents: cobalt chloride, cupric sulfate, nickel chloride, silver nitrate, sodium borate and zinc sulfate. Silver nitrate was the most effective in promoting root branching of woody plant seedlings in a field trial.

Work in Canada and in Ohio has shown that cupric carbonate has been an effective promoter of root regeneration following transplanting. These findings were determined by treating the inside of plastic containers with cupric carbonate.

None of these metal compounds, however, are registered by the Federal Environmental Protection Agency for use in controlling root growth at this time. 🌲

PRUNING
FOR CHARACTER
& SIZE CONTROL

George S. Avery

O n one of our early trips to Japan we visited a rural elementary school on Shodo Island (Shodoshima), in the Inland Sea. It was a memorable visit in more ways than one. Our guide and host was the late Kanichiro Yashiroda, long a Brooklyn Botanic Garden correspondent and personal friend. (Mr. Yashiroda was Guest Editor of several special-subject handbooks, and was twice appointed a Teaching Fellow for courses on bonsai at the Botanic Garden.)

Along with all the warmth and friendliness, there is another outstanding item of memory...a great multiple-trunked tree on the school grounds, a truly venerable specimen. Its character? Three great trunks that leaned out over the school playground. Its age? Probably 250 to 300 years. In richness of appearance and inspiration, it offered something of the spirit of bonsai, though a giant in structure.

I wondered then, and I wonder now,

how it is that we of the Western world have missed seeing and appreciating the grace of wind-blown trees, or the special qualities of asymmetrical balance, or the charm of multiple-trunked trees. "Specimen" trees with their single formal upright trunks have long been the objective of landscapers and others primarily concerned with street and park plantings. But why have the rest of us failed to venture into the less formal patterns that nature offers us for our own home grounds? Individual tastes will differ, but included here are a few examples that suggest an approach to what can be done...by those who wish to test their skill.

As for the qualities in woody plants that favor success in pruning and shaping for character, it is of greatest importance to select species or varieties with fine-textured foliage; large leaves simply are not compatible with attaining quality of skeletal form. If broadleaf deciduous specimens are desired, it is imperative to select varieties whose leaves are naturally small and with short leaf-stalks (petioles). In general, choose species that have only one leaf at a node.

George S. Avery *was Director of the Brooklyn Botanic Garden from 1944 to 1969.*

Examples are small-leaved azaleas and Japanese hornbeam. Or, if evergreens are your choice, choose short-needled Japanese white pine, yew or spruce. Among broadleaf evergreens, several kinds of Japanese holly are ideal candidates.

If starting with younger plants that you might select at a nursery, the trunk can be shaped by pruning. Simply remove the straight upright-growing leader and leave a side branch at the desired height. As the latter grows from year to year, save the branch or branches growing in the direction desired and clip off the others. This is the secret of developing the desired asymmetrical structure, thus determining the form of the tree-to-be.

Foliage masses (clumps of dense foliage) can, in turn, be developed by cutting out some of the branches, leaving open spaces here and there to show portions of the main trunk or more important side branches. At the same time, shorten all lateral branches wherever dense clumps of foliage are desired, cutting each branchlet back to a bud. Later, after the plant is older, one needs only to shear the periphery of the foliage masses to maintain them. Paul Takuma Tono, another Japanese Visiting Fellow at the Botanic Garden some years ago, referred to the foliage masses as simulating "clouds floating in the sky."

Pruning and thinning older specimens of low-growing (dwarf) varieties can often bring surprisingly interesting results in just a few years. But a word of warning: For ease of maintenance of varieties that if left unaltered would grow on into large trees, keep them at a workable height. Six to eight feet should be the maximum. I keep a Swiss stone pine (*Pinus cembra*) at six feet and a Japanese white pine (*P. parviflora*) at eight feet. The latter requires a step ladder for its once a-year grooming. Both trees are something over forty years old...and give me considerable pleasure.

In summary, if one seeks to develop trees of unusual character for special locations or situations, it takes a bit more than orthodox know-how of sanitary pruning and thinning. Highly selective pruning is the answer.

Selective pruning restores open form.

UNSHEARING SHRUBS

Cass Turnbull

First shearing:
Before shearing, branching is open and natural.

Second shearing:
First shearing has provoked growth of many new shoots

Third shearing:
Repeated shearing has produced twiggy canopy. Dense canopy shades interior; leaves and branches die.

ndrea opened my eyes. Years ago when I worked for a city park department, my crew took pride in keeping junipers, dogwoods, spirea and azaleas neatly sheared, and the public complimented us.

Then the department hired Andrea, a horticulturist, to teach us about plants. Observing our careful shearing, she said, "It's a crime against nature."

I was surprised and confused at first, but eventually I understood that selective pruning is better than shearing for most shrubs. It respects their natural form and is less threatening to their health. As a bonus, it is easier on the gardener.

I have to admit that shearing has its place when formality and contrast are important, as in hedges and topiary, and in knot, rose and Japanese gardens.

CASS TURNBULL left Seattle Parks Department in 1986 after 11 years. She operates a landscape business, and is founder of PlantAmnesty, a rapidly growing nonprofit organization dedicated to ending the senseless torture and mutilation of trees and shrubs.

But I don't believe that sheared shrubbery makes a conventional yard look tidy and interesting. To me, it's an eyesore. Sometimes I resort to mockery and call sheared shrubs "poodleballs," "hockey pucks" and "green meatballs."

In my landscaping business, I help gardeners unshear their shrubs. When a client calls, I often find a close-cropped bun of leaves. In a few years, I transform it into an open framework of branches with a graceful, natural-looking canopy. The process takes judicious pruning in small doses. I'll show you how I do it, but first I'll talk about the drawbacks of shearing.

What's Wrong with Shearing?

For one thing, few shrubs are well suited to shearing. The ideal candidate is tough enough to take repeated shearing, and regrows from old branches if you must prune away its leafy shell. The best plants for shearing also have small evergreen leaves, so they look neat and attractive all year.

Among conifers, only fine-needled yews, junipers, hemlocks and arborvitae look tidy when sheared, and only the yew reliably produces new growth when cut back to branches three years old or older.

There are relatively few broadleaf evergreens suitable for shearing; among them are boxwood, Japanese holly, evergreen privet, pyracantha, evergreen azalea and box honeysuckle. All are rugged and small-leaved.

Shearing wastes the beauty of many shrubs. I know gardeners who have never seen their shrubs bloom because they shear them after the flower buds have formed. They could shear after flowering, but they'd have to tolerate shrubs that looked a little long-haired. I'd rather have a graceful shrub with flowers than a formal one without.

In addition, shearing hides or destroys the beautiful bark and branching of plants such as camellia, strawberry tree, azalea, Japanese maple and eastern dogwood (believe it or not, some people in Seattle "lollipop" them).

Branches and flowers aside, shearing also limits the richness of a landscape. Where there could be striking contrasts of texture and form, shearing imposes uniformity. The fine-leaved boxwood and the bold-leaved viburnum lose character when sheared. A weeping Alaska cedar and an angular Pfitzer juniper contrast nicely when you prune naturally, but not when you shear.

Worst of all, shearing locks you into a high-maintenance routine. To explain why, I have to talk about the two basic pruning cuts: thinning and heading.

When you prune a branch back to its parent branch or to the ground, you make a thinning cut. When you shorten a branch by pruning anywhere between its tip and its base, you make a heading cut.

Since heading almost always encourages shoots to grow rapidly from the remaining buds and twigs on the branch, and often prompts dormant buds to produce shoots as well, you soon get a crowd of new shoots around a heading cut.

Shearing is basically wholesale heading. So year by year, a sheared shrub grows a little larger and a lot twiggier (see the drawings).

New shoots grow rapidly after shearing, as the shrub replaces lost leaves. Within weeks or months, you have to shear again.

Furthermore, shearing threatens a shrub's health. As a shrub hastens to replace lost leaves, it expends energy reserves to produce rapidly growing new shoots which are susceptible to drought, cold, pests and diseases.

Many shrubs lack the stamina to rebound. Barberry and spirea, for example, develop dead spots with repeated shearing. Vigorous shrubs tolerate shearing, but they still suffer stress.

The dense canopy resulting from shearing shades a shrub's interior. For lack of sunlight, a leafless zone develops, and eventually twigs die. Meanwhile, fallen leaves catch in the branches, making "bird's nests" that invite pests and diseases.

Unshearing

How do you restore sheared shrubs to their natural shape?

Have the right gear when you start. Use a good pair of bypass shears, the kind with curved blades that slide past each other. They cut cleanly and leave no stub when you cut a branch at the base. Have a pair of loppers and a pruning saw on hand, too. I like the small saws with folding blades. They fit in a pocket, and work in tight quarters. I usually wear leather gloves — sheared shrubs are scratchy.

Thin selectively, removing some of the twiggy canopy each year, and let time do the rest. You can unshear at any time of the year. I divide shrubs into two basic categories and prune them differently.

Plants in the one group, which I call cane-growers, make a cluster of stems that branch very little, if at all; forsythias are representatives of this category.

The other group have a few main stems, and most branches rebranch repeatedly; deciduous azaleas are a good example. Let's call these the much-branched shrubs, and discuss them later.

Unshearing Cane-Growers

Cane-growers are tough and renew themselves readily from the base. I restore them by cutting a few stems off at the base and thinning a little each year, or by drastic renovation.

Cane-growers are easier to unshear than much-branched shrubs are. Each year, you remove a few of the biggest, oldest stems, cutting them as close as possible to the crown of the plant or to the ground. If loppers won't work, use the pruning saw. Also look in the canopy for the most snarled, twiggiest branches and cut them back to a side branch or bud, preferably one that faces outward so new growth will leave the interior open.

Remove no more than one-third of the canopy each year. If you take too much, many plants try to recoup by suckering profusely from the ground and sprouting from the remaining branches. The new shoots grow rapidly and make a bigger pruning job the next year.

For some very old shrubs, radical renovation may be in order. It's a drastic treatment — rather than thinning gradually for several years, you cut the shrub clear to the ground all at once.

Only tough deciduous cane-growing shrubs, such as forsythia, philadelphus, deutzia, kolkwitzia and potentilla, tolerate radical renovation; they resprout readily from the crown and roots. Keep in mind that a cut back shrub needs three years or more to look good again and to flower.

[Ed. note: In general, total renovation is best done in late winter or early spring before new growth starts, when carbohydrate reserves in roots are high. For more on renovation, also called rejuvenation, see "Pruning Deciduous and Needled Evergreen Shrubs," on page 36.]

Unshearing Much-Branched Shrubs

With much-branched shrubs, the hardest part is getting started. You can take three approaches: Snip a lot of twigs; thin small branches; or cut out the worst twiggy clumps. I recommend that you combine all three practices, but concentrate on the last.

First, choose a portion of the canopy about a foot square. Then run a hand over it, feeling for the thickest clump of twigs. Push the clump aside to see how it branches, and prune it off with a thinning cut as the drawings illustrate.

Proceed around the canopy, section by section. Thin equally for the most part, but a bit more heavily around the base of the shrub than on the top to soften the look of a box, ball or bun. Finish the whole canopy this way. Then go back over it a square foot at a time, cutting out a few crossing twigs and small weak branches, and call it a day.

When you step back for a look, be prepared to see very little change. Heavily-sheared shrubs need time to resume natural shapes. Where you remove clumps the first year, nearby branches spring into the gap. Resist the urge to keep pruning. On many shrubs, heavy thinning invites trouble. If you remove more than one-third of the canopy at a time, you stress the shrub and provoke it into producing rapidly growing shoots.

The next year, prune again. Take out the worst clumps and branches as you did the first year, and look for new growth that needs thinning. With light reaching

Shearing produces a temporarily tidy effect, but new shoots often grow vigorously, as shown here, and soon the shrub needs shearing again.

the shrub's interior for the first time in years, long-dormant buds come to life. This new growth will give you something to cut back to in the future if you choose to reduce the size of your shrub.

The sheared silhouette eventually breaks up. By the second year, the base of the shrub opens a little, and the canopy shows rolling contours. By the third year, the original layer of twigs is

Repeated shearing develops a dense canopy of leaves and twigs, as shown here. The shrub's natural shape gives way to a geometric silhouette, with all the branches hidden.

almost gone, and the shrub is evolving a natural pattern of branches.

The interior of a sheared shrub needs work, too. With big shrubs, I like to get inside the canopy and work up and out from the bottom. Whether you work from the inside or the outside, clean out leaves hung up in the forks of branches, and prune off all dead branches.

Remove any branch that grows inward through the center and out the other side. Cut out the worst of the branches that cross or rub other branches. As you thin wayward branches, step back frequently to check your progress. It's easy to cut too much. Heed the old saying, "Wander, ponder and prune."

A Final Plea

I hope I've persuaded you to prune rather than shear. But if you're not swayed yet, consider two last points. Sheared shrubs get bigger every year and eventually outgrow their site. If the shrub will regrow from old branches, you can cut if back drastically. You'll soon face the challenge of pruning a forest of vigorous new shoots, however. By contrast, if you prune shrubs to natural shapes, you can control their growth with a few thinning cuts.

Pruning selectively is a lot less work than shearing. Some species, sheared, need several "mowings" per year to maintain formal rigidity.

When shrubs and trees are pruned for the "natural look," an hour a year will take care of most yards. Wouldn't you like to use the time you spend shearing to enjoy healthy, naturally shaped shrubs instead? ✂

The sequence of drawings below shows how to restore a sheared shrub to a natural open form, using thinning cuts and removing a third or less of the canopy each year. Cut crowded older branches and twiggy clumps, like the one in the first drawing at right, back to side branches. Thin new branches, shown here in green, by pruning them off at the the base. (Pruned branches are indicated in gray.) Note that in the three years, the number of branches in the canopy drops by half. As the canopy loosens, clean up the interior of the shrub by removing lodged leaves and pruning dead branches.

First year:
Remove thickest clumps by cutting back to side branches. Thin shoots and trim stubs left by shearing.

Second year:
Continue to open canopy by cutting back old branches to side branches and thinning new growth.

Third year:
Shrub is regaining natural open form. Continue to thin old and new growth.

PRUNING ROSES

PETER MALINS

&

STEPHEN SCANNIELLO

All roses need pruning. If roses aren't pruned for a number of years, plants deteriorate in appearance and often develop more disease and insect problems, while the flowers become smaller and smaller.

HYBRID TEA, GRANDIFLORA AND FLORI-BUNDA ROSES require annual pruning in the spring after winter protection has been removed. There is an old saying that roses are pruned when the forsythia blooms. In the New York metropolitan region, this is late March or early April. In other areas, rose pruning time will vary according to climate; check with your local rose society. If rosebushes are pruned too early, injury from repeated frost may make a second pruning necessary.

TOOLS AND SUPPLIES. For small pruning jobs, the only tools necessary are sharp pruning shears — the scissor-type

secateurs are best — and gloves. If the rose collection is larger, a small saw with pointed blade and loppers will help. Loppers are used to reach in and cut out large dead canes.

To discourage borers, apply Elmer's Glue or similar white glue to seal the cuts. Where roses are infected with brown canker, carry a can of denatured alcohol to sterilize shears after each cut.

REASONS FOR PRUNING. Prune to remove branches that are dead, damaged, diseased, thin, weak and growing inward, and branches that cross or interfere with other branches. This encourages new growth from the base, making the plant healthier and more attractive and resulting in larger blossoms.

PRUNING STEPS. Remove all dead and diseased wood by cutting at least one inch below the damaged area. Remove the entire cane if it's dead.

Remove all weak shoots. If two branches rub or are close enough that they will do so soon, remove one. On

PETER MALINS is the former rosarian and STEPHEN SCANNIELLO the current rosarian of the Brooklyn Botanic Garden's Cranford Rose Garden.

older, heavy bushes, cut out one or two of the oldest canes each year.

Cut back the remaining canes, The height to which a rose should be cut back will vary depending upon the normal habit of the particular bush and the personal preference of the gardener. The average pruning height for Floribundas and Hybrid Teas is between 12 and 18 inches, but taller-growing hybrids such as Grandifloras may be left at two feet.

Make cuts at a 45 degree angle above a strong outer bud. Aim the cut upward from the inner side of the bush to push growth outward and promote healthy shoots and quality flowers.

MINIATURE ROSES. Miniatures are roses with tiny blooms and foliage. Miniature roses do not need special pruning. Cut out dead growth and thin the centers. Miniature roses can also be pruned to maintain a shape or height.

RAMBLERS. The old-fashioned Rambler roses have clusters of flowers, each flower usually less than two inches across. They often produce pliable canes 10 to 15 feet long in one season. Ramblers produce best on year-old wood, so that this year's choice blooms come on last year's growth. Prune immediately after flowering.

In summer, remove entirely some of the larger old canes after flowering. Tie new canes to a support for the next year.

LARGE-FLOWERING CLIMBERS. The canes of these roses are larger and sturdier than those of the Ramblers. Some flower just once at the beginning of the season, but some, called ever-blooming climbers, flower more or less continuously. They should be pruned once the rose is dormant. First cut out dead and diseased canes. Then, one or two of the oldest canes may be removed each season at ground level to make room for new canes. The laterals, or side shoots, should be shortened three to six inches after flowering. If the plant is strong, keep five to eight main canes, which should be tied to the trellis, fence or other support.

PRUNING IS AN ART. Prune with common sense. No particular technique is the only correct one. Any good rose gardener will find his own method. Pruning becomes an art, and you will learn from experience just how each plant should be handled. If you make a mistake, the plant will not die, and in time you will discover just what will produce the most and the best blooms. 🌹

Buds breaking in the spring.

New growth on spring-pruned canes.

Using sharp pruning shears, cut at a 45° angle just above an outer bud.

A bed of rose bushes before pruning in the spring.

The same bed of roses after spring pruning.

PRUNING HERBACEOUS PLANTS

Tracy DiSabato-Aust

Pruning is a practice normally associated with woody plants, but it also has broad application to herbaceous plants. When you deadhead, pinch, disbud or cut back herbaceous plants, you are pruning them.

Deadheading means removing flowers, one at a time or in clusters, which have faded or died. Many species will either flower for a longer period or rebloom if deadheaded.

Early bloomers such as pansies, and a host of summer flowering species and cultivars will keep blossoming far longer if deadheaded regularly.

Tidiness, too, is vastly improved by plucking spent flowers of some plants, especially daylilies.

Deadheading also can prevent self-seeding, which in the case of cultivars may result in inferior seedlings the next season (many cultivars do not "come true" from self-seeding). Columbines are particularly heavy seeders, and will come up even in gravel driveways if they're not deadheaded before going to seed.

TRACY DISABATO-AUST *is a horticultural consultant, designer, writer and lecturer from Sunbury, Ohio. She has worked, studied and taught at arboreta in Belgium, England, Canada, and the U.S.*

Of course, you may opt against deadheading plants that produce ornamental seed heads after flowering.

If flowers appear at ends or among leaves of leafy stems (e.g. pansies, petunias), deadheading consists of plucking spent flowers or flower clusters.

To deadhead plants that have foliage at the bases of flower stalks, prune off stalks just above the foliage or just above new flower buds (e.g. shasta daisies, salvia, yarrow).

If plants have bare flower stems (e.g. hostas, daylilies, most spring bulbs), cut them just above ground level.

Spring flowering bulbs should be deadheaded before going to seed. Plants will look better, and the bulbs will store more energy for next year's blossoming. Prune old flower stalks as close to their points of origin as possible.

A deadheading technique that is akin to pinching (see below) is the removal of flowers as they form in order to promote foliage. This is beneficial to colorful ornamental plants such as coleus, and to herbs grown for culinary foliage, such as basil, oregano and the mints.

Pinching is removing about half an inch of growing tip. This creates bushier and more compact plants and decreases the need for staking. Pinched plants will generally have more, but smaller, flowers.

Many annuals benefit from pinching at planting time. The resulting plants are sturdier, bushier and more floriferous.

Similarly, many late summer and autumn flowering plants benefit from pinching.

Chrysanthemums give best fall displays if pinched, starting in spring when growth is six or so inches high and continuing every two weeks until July 15 in the Midwest. Most cultivars of Michaelmas daisies benefit from a couple of early pinchings.

Because pinching tends to delay flowering, a bed of one species or cultivar may be enticed to show color for longer than normal periods. For example, pinch one third of the plants in the bed well before normal blooming time. A week later, pinch another one third and pinch the rest another week later.

Disbudding is removal of superfluous flower buds only, long before blooming. If side buds are removed and only the terminal bud is left, results are a much larger flower and a longer stem. If the main bud is removed, side shoots will produce more, but smaller, flowers.

Disbudding is usually used by exhibitors and/or flower arrangers with plants such as chrysanthemums, dahlias, carnations and peonies.

Cutting back is the relatively severe practice of removing one-third or more of the upper portions of plants in one courageous swoop.

Many low-growing spring-flowering rock garden plants and edging plants should be cut back by one-half after flowering. Examples are evergreen candytuft, moss phlox, rock cress and snow-in-summer. Some gardeners cheat at this chore by using a string trimmer. Taller plants that benefit from cutting back after flowering are *Veronica latifolia* , catmint and spiderwort.

Some normally tall growers, such as great blue lobelia, ironweed, boneset and native asters, may also be cut back long before flowering, by half when plants are four inches tall and again when 12 to 16 inches high.

Perennials with one heavy bloom period, including golden marguerite, lilyleaf ladybells and painted daisies, should be cut back by one-third after flowering simply to keep plants tidy.

Annuals such as petunias and impatiens may become leggy and disheveled

Before: New growth emerging from base of delphinium.

After removing old foliage new growth buds begin to form.

by midsummer. Enthusiastic cutting back will revive them for a late summer show.

A good haircut during the heat of summer does wonders for the ground cover plant known as bishop's weed or goutweed.

Some plants, such as bee balm and 'Alaska' shasta daisy, produce new growth at ground level in late summer, when shabby bloomed-out upper portions may be cut back to the new growth.

And at the end of the season as winter approaches, foliage of most herbaceous perennials should be cut to the ground and removed from the garden. This spruces up the garden and reduces chances of insects overwintering in dead leaves and stems.

Exceptions to prewinter whacking are evergreens such as sea pinks, European ginger, evergreen candytuft, *Sedum spurium* and some of the ferns. ❀

Cut back *Anthemis tinctoria* by one third after flowering.

Lobelia siphilitica was pinched back two months ago.

Pruning *Anthemis tinctoria*.

71

HEDGE PRUNING

BASICS

JAMES A. MACK

Hedges, like other ornamental plantings, have function as well as beauty in the landscape. Hedges dictate traffic flow, frame attractive views, screen undesirable views and define space.

I have seen examples of both magnificent and extremely poor hedges over the years. Several variables determine success or failure with hedges. Perhaps the most important step (after site preparation and planting) is to start them off from the very beginning with sound pruning and shaping.

Even the best choice of plants in an ideal location will make a mediocre hedge — or worse — with inadequate early training.

Formal Versus Informal Hedges

Formal hedges, composed of hard, crisp lines, are often used to complement geometric architectural shapes, to define spaces sharply, to provide backdrops for smaller, showy plants or to screen undesirable views. Deciduous or evergreen,

JAMES A. MACK, *educated in horticulture at Cornell University and in the Longwood Graduate Program, University of Delaware, is Superintendent of Grounds for the Holden Arboretum, Mentor, Ohio.*

formal hedges are usually grown for quality of foliage, not flowers.

Informal hedges may serve several of the same purposes. However, they are often grown primarily for ornamental flowers, and secondarily for foliage. Informal hedges are best used free-standing to offer full appreciation of seasonal beauty.

First-Year Pruning

Too often a novice gardener will plant a hedge with the intent of forming a tall hedge in the shortest possible time. The result is a spindly hedge, sparsely branched and inadequately clothed with foliage, especially at the base.

It's important to spend enough time during the first three or four years properly training the plants to grow into attractive and functional hedges.

Initial pruning is aimed at restricting top growth to encourage side branching at the base.

Leaves need sufficient light to sustain them. Shading of lower limbs by upper ones, due to improper pruning (or lack of pruning) results in top-heavy hedges with most of the foliage in the upper half or one-third of the plants.

To avoid this, always prune hedges

wider at the base than at the top. This allows light to reach all the leaves and encourages branching and foliage clear to the ground.

In regions with moderate to heavy snowfall, it is wise to round the top surface or even taper it to a blunt point. This aids in shedding of snow before it can build up and damage the hedge.

Directly after planting deciduous hedges (both formal and informal), string a line (using two or more stakes) parallel to the ground along the hedge. The height of the line should be midway between the shortest and tallest plants.

Prune ("tip out") upright branches of the taller plants down to the vicinity of the string. Cut branches cleanly just above side-branch junctions, or just above obvious dormant buds. Make slightly slanting cuts about one-fourth inch above side branches or buds that remain.

Allow plants below the string to produce upright growth till they reach the height of the other plants before tipping them out.

After pruning upper shoots of the taller plants, clip back side branches of all plants, removing no more than one-half of their lengths, to loosely approximate a pyramidal shape.

Do not prune back needleleaf or broadleaf evergreens, usually used for formal hedges, as hard as deciduous plants. But the basic shaping process applies, especially to overly-long side shoots.

In all cases, it's best to use scissors-type

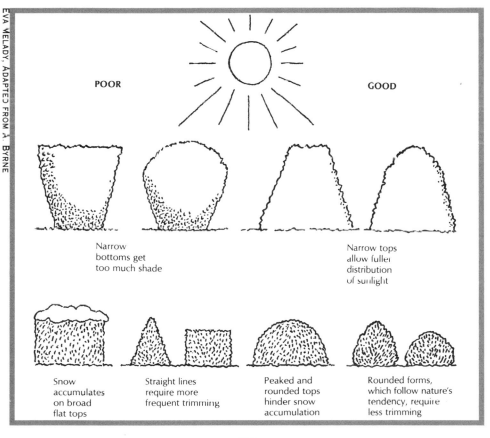

POOR   GOOD

Narrow bottoms get too much shade

Narrow tops allow fuller distribution of sunlight

Snow accumulates on broad flat tops

Straight lines require more frequent trimming

Peaked and rounded tops hinder snow accumulation

Rounded forms, which follow nature's tendency, require less trimming

Blue beech (*Carpinus caroliniana*) makes a fine deciduous hedge.

Hemlock hedge (*Tsuga canadensis*) trimmed so that the base is wider than the top.

hand shears to assure clean and well-placed cuts.

Second Year and Beyond Formal Hedges

During second and subsequent growing seasons, formal hedges, whether evergreen or deciduous, should be allowed to proceed slowly to their ultimate heights via regular pruning.

Each shaping should remove no more than one-half of new shoot growth. Most evergreen hedges, needle or broadleaf, will need only one pruning in midsummer.

Deciduous types, especially fast-growing species like privet (*Ligustrum*), may need monthly pruning to maintain proper density of branching.

In colder climates (winters with temperatures often below freezing), avoid pruning hedges after mid August. Later pruning may encourage soft new growth that won't have time to harden off before winter.

Informal Hedges

Informal hedges, as a rule, can be left mostly to their own devices during their second season, with spot pruning here and there to head back occasional rampant shoots.

An exception is when low side branches do not develop satisfactorily. If this is the case, shorten terminal shoots by one-half, to encourage development of basal branches.

Once a good base is developed, an informal hedge should be shaped only when necessary, and allowed to grow mostly naturally to its full ornamental potential.

Maintaining Hedges

Once a hedge has developed fully into the desired shape and size, the amount of maintenance pruning will be dictated by the growth characteristics of the species and the tastes of the gardener. Usually, timely attention once a year will suffice.

Be forewarned that formal hedges of some species will not tolerate pruning away of outer foliage; bare inner branches thus exposed may not leaf out again. Other species, such as the evergreen yews (*Taxus*) and most deciduous plants, will sprout readily from older wood.

When to prune is an important consideration for informal flowering hedges. Spring-flowering species, such as forsythia, mock orange (*Philadelphus*) and lilacs (*Syringa*), will not flower to their full potential if pruned in the dormant season before flowering. For maximum blossoming, prune these species just after flowering.

Summer-flowering species, such as sweet pepperbush (*Clethra alnifolia*), abelia and rose-of-sharon (*Hibiscus syriacus*), are best pruned in winter or early spring before new spring growth.

Pruning Tools for Hedges

I am often asked which pruning tools are best for hedges.

For informal hedges, deciduous or evergreen, I prefer a scissors-type hand pruner. Though it may take a bit longer, pruning with this tool allows carefully chosen cuts to be made, minimizing damage to foliage, especially on broadleaf evergreens such as rhododendron and holly (*Ilex*).

Formal hedges can be trimmed with either power trimmers or manual hedge shears. Manual shears deliver cleaner cuts, minimizing chewing of leaves and twigs. Electric or gasoline powered trimmers are faster, and if cutting edges are sharp and the operator is skillful, will do a neat job on fine-textured plants such as yews, abelia, privet and hemlock (*Tsuga*).

Following basic procedures for pruning can establish and maintain beautiful, functional hedges for many years to come. ⬥

Taxus hedge defines a wavy margin.

Korean boxwood trimmed so that the top is rounded to shed snow.

MOWING

IS PRUNING, TOO

Eliot C. Roberts

Fertilization, pest control, aeration of the root-zone when necessary, irrigation and mowing are all important lawn care practices. The last two are the most important and often determine the success or failure of the other cultural endeavors.

Importance of Mowing

Mowing is particularly important. Not only does clipping height influence turf grass vigor and persistence, but clipping frequency determines the amount of foliage removed at one time and thus influences the rate of regrowth as well as the need to bag and remove grass clippings from the site.

Mulching mowers chop leaf segments into tiny pieces that sift out of sight into turf, negating need for removal of clippings (and, contrary to popular opinion, the pulverized clippings do not cause thatch).

EDITOR'S NOTE: Several states now have regulations that ban clippings, leaves and other plant materials in landfills.

In general, mowing at any given height should be done often enough so as to clip no more than one-third of the grass height at any one time. E.g., if grass

DR. ELIOT C. ROBERTS, *soil scientist and turf specialist, has served on university faculties in Massachusetts, Iowa, Rhode Island, and Florida. He has written more than 200 technical papers and popular articles. Currently, Roberts is Executive Director of the Lawn Institute, Pleasant Hill, Tennessee.*

is to be cut to two inches, it should be mowed when it reaches three inches. Thus, one inch, which is one-third of the height when mowed, is removed.

If grass is to be cut to one inch, it should be mowed when it grows to one and a half inches, so one-half inch is removed.

It follows that mowing frequency should be doubled when mowing height is halved.

Mowing height and frequency can and should be adjusted in accordance with the growth of the turf. Heat, cold, moisture, drought, nitrogen fertilization and many other cultural practices influence the rate of lawn grass growth and development. These conditions create stress or relieve stress within the turf. Mowing must not create more stress in plants that are already weakened.

Adjustment and operating conditions of mowing equipment become very important in these instances. Reels and bed knives on reel mowers and cutting blades on rotary mowers must be sharp and well adjusted. Cleanly cut grass blades heal quickly with little damage to the plants.

Considerable research has been conducted on the need for mowing in the development and maintenance of fine turf. This practice is necessary to cause tillering (growth of new shoots from the base of a grass plant) so that turf density is increased. A good tight turf is not only pleasing to look at, it also helps prevent weed seedlings from getting started. Grass should occupy space needed by weeds and actually crowd them out.

There is a limit to how low a given turf should be cut. Below the optimum height of cut, too little leaf surface is available for photosynthesis and a weakened turf results. Density lessens and the turf cover opens up to expose soil. Weeds become established more readily. Root zones of turf grasses shrink under these conditions as roots die back and are replaced by regrowth. In effect, cutting too low reduces organic food substances and the turf suffers malnutrition. Under extreme conditions, such grass may starve to death.

Raising the height of cut allows more leaf surface and creates at least the potential for recovery and resumed health and vigor.

Even small increases in cutting height produce dramatic increases in total leaf surface, which in turn increase vigor of the grass. For most grass species, raising mower blades just one-eighth inch from minimal cutting height results in the equivalent of more than 300 square feet of leaf surface per 1,000 square feet!

One-fourth inch more cutting height gives 600 to 900 more square feet of leaf surface per 1,000 square feet; one-half inch higher, from 1,250 to 1,800 more square feet of lawn equivalent.

Mowing Heights

Each lawn grass cultivar has a recommended clipping height which will make it most vigorous and healthy. These heights vary from less than one-fourth inch for creeping bentgrasses on golf greens to about three inches for some of the coarser, non-spreading type grasses. Reel mowers are best suited for close cutting and rotary mowers do a good job at clipping heights from one and one-half to three inches. Lawn grasses cut much above three inches fail to form a nice uniform, close knit turf.

Grasses for Cool, Humid Regions

KENTUCKY BLUEGRASSES — on the average, Kentucky bluegrasses should be mowed at about one and one-half inches. All natural types do best at this height of cut. Some new, named cultivars have a minimum mowing height of about one inch. Follow instructions on the seed container.

FINE FESCUES — including red fescue, creeping fescue, Chewings fescue and hard fescue, should be mowed at one and one-half inches. Actually, these grasses will tolerate clipping at one-half inch or lower when free of competition from more vigorous grasses. In partial shade (no grass will grow in full shade), elevation of the clipping height to two inches is good practice.

TURF-TYPE PERENNIAL RYEGRASSES — form a good solid turf when clipped at two inches. Many of the new named cultivars have been bred to tolerate a one-inch height. On lawns and sports turf, mowing from one to two inches high is about right.

TURF-TYPE TALL FESCUE — the old cultivars of turf-type tall fescue require a clipping height of about three inches. Newer cultivars perform best when cut at two inches. Now there are new dwarf cultivars that can tolerate clipping as low as one inch. Check the seed container for clipping height for your selection. In general, these grasses perform well when cut higher than the minimum specified.

COLONIAL BENT AND CREEPING BENT GRASSES — are the closest clipped of the cool season grasses. Creeping bent grasses used on golf courses are not recommended for home lawns. They require too much care.

Colonial bent grass cultivars look best when mowed from one-half to one inch high. Sow these with fine fescue (25% bent grass and 75% fine fescue) and mow the mixture at one inch.

GRASS MIXTURES — Most lawns in northern, cool, humid regions are mixtures of two or more different grasses. Each of these will have a preference for height of cut. By raising or lowering the height during the growing season, it is possible to encourage one grass at the expense of another. In general, mow at a height that will favor that grass or those grasses most desirable in creating the quality of lawn desired.

EDITOR'S NOTE: Many authorities in Ohio and neighboring states recommend cutting most mixtures at two and one-half inches, especially if they are not irrigated.

Southern grasses used in the warm, humid regions of the country are generally not planted as mixtures but are grown as monocultures.

Grasses for Warm Regions

BERMUDA GRASSES — are the closet cut of the southern grasses. They are used on golf greens and will tolerate a cut of one-fourth inch or less. For lawns, bermuda grasses should be mowed at heights of from one-half to one inch.

ZOYSIA GRASSES — get soft and spongy when mowed much above one inch. They perform best when cut close to keep thatch from forming and when top-dressed to maintain a firm surface.

ST. AUGUSTINE GRASSES — are usually cut higher in the Upper South (up to three inches) and lower through southern Florida and along the Gulf Coast (down to one inch). These grasses tend to get soft and thatchy when cut high, necessitating thatch control.

CENTIPEDE GRASSES — make nice looking lawns when mowed at about one and one-half inches.

BAHIA GRASSES — are open in habit of growth and make a second-rate turf at best. Bahia grass lawns look best when clipped at three inches.

BUFFALO GRASSES — make an attractive dry-land turf where lack of water precludes better grasses when cut at from two to three inches. 🌿

Kentucky bluegrass clipped at 1/4, 3/4 and 1-1/2 inches is compared with bluegrass not mowed to see the effect of mowing on root development. Clipping much below 1-1/2 inches restricts root growth so much that Kentucky bluegrass suffers, particularly during summer drought.

ESPALIERS

Alan D. Cook

An espalier plant is one trained to grow flat against a wall, trellis, fence or other support. In the old European and English traditions, branches were trained to symmetrical and often intricate geometric patterns (Fig. 1). Modern styles, while ignoring symmetry, achieve graceful balance through sweeps and curves as well as random patterns (Fig. 2).

Espaliers make great conversation pieces, but they also can do many horticultural jobs. An eighteen-inch strip of soil between a walk and a garage wall is a spot that calls for a shrub or small tree that's trained tall and wide and very thin. Patio boundaries are amenable to trellis-supported espaliers. Stone walls are often better dressed with flat-trained evergreens than with rampant vines.

Espaliers also can feature flowers followed often by fruits or berries, and a fence-supported orchard of espaliered dwarf fruits can produce gratifying harvests in very small spaces. Never remove the short fruiting spurs along the branches of fruit trees, unless they become too thick — that is, closer than two or three inches apart.

A Few Things to Keep in Mind

❶ On walls, north and east exposures minimize winter damage, but some plants won't get enough light on north walls to perform satisfactorily.

❷ Select proper plants for the location. A rhododendron or dogwood, which is shade tolerant, might be suitable for a north wall, but only in well drained, slightly acid soil. Thorny plants would not be desirable beside a walk. Large areas need fast-growing plants. Be sure the plant is perfectly hardy in your climate. Espaliering is time-consuming; gambling with "iffy" plants is better left to conventional culture.

❸ Have a definite design in mind and work toward it from the start. Unless, of course, some other design seems better as the original one develops or falters.

❹ Heavy yearly pruning is usually best done in early spring, or, on spring-blooming plants, immediately after flowering. Touch-up grooming should take place as often as necessary to maintain desired neatness.

❺ As a rule, side shoots should be allowed to grow to about 12 inches before shortening, and a few leaves should be left after pruning. Branches that are a part of the pattern should be tip-trimmed only after they reach desired length.

❻ Think about methods of attachment. On masonry, drill holes and cement in rustproof hooks or eyes.

Against wood construction, trellises are advisable for support. Metal rods welded together make fine trellises.

❼ Use soft material for tying branches to supports. Pieces of insulated copper wire, soft cord or even strips of lead can be used for this purpose. Check the attachments twice a year and loosen them as necessary to prevent constriction of growth.

Suggested Plants

Almost any woody plant can be used for the purpose, but some are superior. A partial list includes: flowering quince, flowering dogwood, cotoneaster, hawthorn, euonymus, forsythia, American holly, magnolia, apple and crabapple, cherries, flowering cherries, plums, pears, pyracantha, yews and viburnum. 🐾

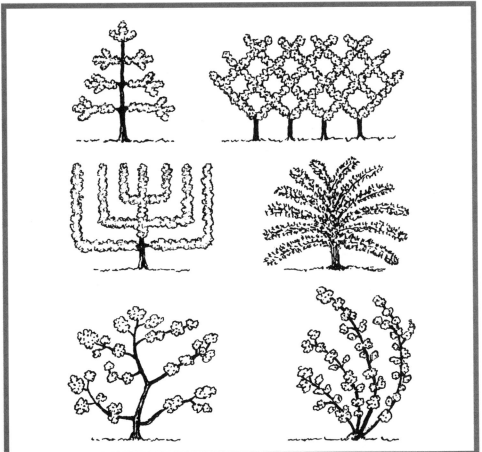

DRAWING BY ALAN D. COOK

Top and center: Espaliering single or multiple plants can be simple or intricate. Training must start when plants are young and supple.
Bottom: Modern, more casual espaliers of flower arrangement patterns.

LIVING SCULPTURE AT LONGWOOD GARDENS

PAM ALLENSTEIN

Topiary is a highly individual art form, a kind of living sculpture. Marray's New English Dictionary of 1928 defines topiary as "the art of cutting trees and shrubs into quaint devices." The art of topiary has roots in the classical Greek and Roman period. Through the centuries, topiary as a horticultural art form has been developed by the French, Dutch, English and more recently the Ecuadoreans and the Americans.

The Topiary Garden at Longwood Gardens in Pennsylvania was started in 1936 by Pierre S. du Pont with eleven large rounds, four cones and a horseshoe-shaped hedge to accent an Analemmatic sundial. In 1958 thirty more figures were introduced from the Bismark Estate in Bayville, Long Island, with later additions from an Illinois nursery (Charles Fiore, Prairie View), Taylor Arboretum in Pennsylvania and Longwood's own nursery.

The current display features massive geometric figures, cones, spirals, a pyramid, "cake-stands" topped with birds, a chair and table and several animals. Located in a sunken garden surrounded by stone walls and hedges, the topiaries are protected from drying winds while enjoying a sunny exposure.

The actual mechanics of pruning the topiary figures is much like clipping hedges. In the past gardeners at Longwood used hand clippers to prune the topiary. Gardeners currently use electric hedge shears for the annual summer shearing. Hand pruners are used to remove knots, and for cleaning and deadwooding in the late winter. A battery-powered hydraulic lift replaces boards and scaffolding once used to reach the tops of the taller pieces. Today's approach emphasizes safety. Gardeners are required to wear gloves, eye protection and earplugs or earphones to muffle the sound of noisy shears.

Topiary gardening requires an extra dose of patience. Gardeners must pay close attention to detail in line, proportion and symmetry. The topiary figures at Longwood are cut free form. Occasionally, templates, plumb lines, strings or measuring sticks are used to make corrections or adjustments to the geometric shapes. Not using frames allows gardeners the flexibility to alter a shape if

PAMELA ALLENSTEIN *is in charge of the Topiary Garden at Longwood Gardens. She recently completed her M.S. in Public Horticulture Administration through the Longwood Graduate Program.*

Longwood Gardens has a large collection of topiary.

desired. Each topiary "artist" may contribute to the development of topiary specimens through his or her imagination and skills. Record-keeping and sketches help to "pass on the legacy" through generations of gardeners.

TOPIARY THE EASY WAY

In olden days, a shrub pruned into a bird was shear artistry, carefully crafted by a talented and patient person with pruners.

Now, we can put a wire mesh cage of desired design over a small plant, blithely lop off anything that grows through the mesh, and eventually create a topiary.

Some mail-order sources of topiary frames:

GARDEN MAGIC
2001 1/2 Fairview Road
Raleigh, NC 27608
(919) 833-7315 (free catalog)

KENNETH LYNCH & SONS, INC.
84 Danbury Road
Wilton, CT 06897
(203) 762-8363 (catalog of 10,000 garden items, $8)

TOPIARY, INC.
41 Bering
Tampa, FL 33606
(813) 254-3229 (free catalog free)

VINE ARTS
PO Box 83014
Portland, OR 97203-0014
(503) 289-7505 (catalog, $2)

Pruning is done twice yearly with power equipment and a hydraulic lift.

Although many plants can be used for topiary, the specimens in Longwood's Topiary Garden are several varieties of yew (*Taxus* spp.). Yew responds well to hard pruning and grows at a moderate rate. The natural habits of various varieties — low and spreading or mounded and upright — help determine which variety will lend itself best to a particular shape. Longwood's topiaries are pruned generally once a year, from June through August. More detailed figures and those in prominent positions may be groomed several times during the season. Any major changes are made in the late winter or early spring when new growth can quickly fill in bare patches.

Theories on pruning techniques and timing differ with the particular plant used, growing conditions, availability of time and labor and the judgment of the individual gardener. It is important to prune back to last year's cuts, if you don't want the figure to increase in size. In colder climates, another crucial step is keeping the topiaries free from snow and ice, which can spoil the shape and even damage major limbs.

In addition to Longwood's Topiary Garden near Kennett Square, Pennsylvania, there are three other excellent topiary displays in the Northeast: Ladew Gardens in Monkton, Maryland, Green Animals in Portsmouth, Rhode Island, and Colonial Williamsburg in Williamsburg, Virginia. These gardens display some of the best examples of living sculpture in the country.

LADEW TOPIARY GARDENS FOUNDATION
3535 Jarrettsville Pike
Monkton, MD 21111
(301) 557-9466

GREEN ANIMALS
The Preservation Society of Newport County
118 Mill Street
Newport, RI 02840
(401) 847-1000

COLONIAL WILLIAMSBURG
Drawer C
Williamsburg, VA 23187
(804) 229-1000

LONGWOOD GARDENS, INC.
P.O. Box 501
Kennett Square, PA 19348-0501
(215) 388-6741

PRUNING

&

TRAINING BONSAI

Arthur O. Patznick

Bonsai is the ancient Far Eastern art of dwarfing and training plants to represent trees in their natural environments.

Top Pruning and Training

Before starting to prune and train a bonsai, one should study the plant in question and decide what style the finished bonsai is to be — upright, leaning, cascading or other style.

When starting a new bonsai, or when renovating an older specimen that has been neglected, drastic pruning is in order. Many branches may be removed and most or all remaining branches thinned and shortened. The main trunk may be shortened as well.

Experience is desirable and courage is essential for a grower performing drastic pruning. The framework to be left, a mere skeleton of the plant prior to pruning, depends on the chosen style.

Arthur O. Patznick, *Superintendent of The Dawes Arboretum, Newark, Ohio, was trained in bonsai by Frank Okamura at Brooklyn Botanic Garden in 1968. Since then, Patznick has taught numerous bonsai classes and workshops and organized the Ohio Regional Bonsai Show.*

Drastic pruning is best performed when plants are dormant, prior to the beginning of new growth.

Once a style is chosen and initial drastic pruning accomplished, a bonsai can be trained into full beauty by yearly pruning.

The best time to prune deciduous species is after new shoots have fully developed, but not matured.

The same is true for evergreens other than pines, spruces and firs, which should be pruned by pinching off one-third to two-thirds of "candles" of new growth before they expand fully.

Pinching with thumb and forefinger is suggested; cutting with shears leaves blunt, unattractive needles at the points of pruning.

General Rules for Pruning Bonsai

If two or more branches close together are growing in the same direction, leave only one, usually the smallest.

If two branches cross, one must go.

Remove branches that grow inward.

If one branch is directly above another, chances are one must be removed. Which one depends on the chosen style.

Make all cuts cleanly, with sharp tools

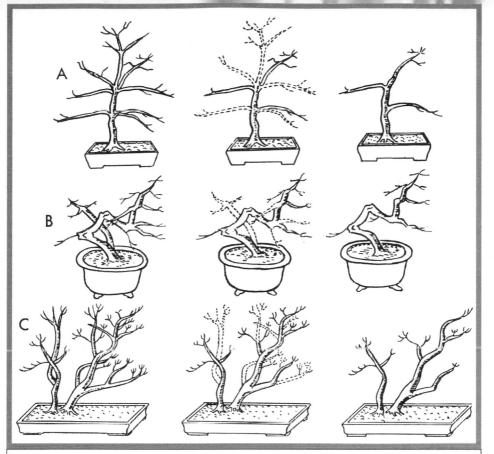

PRUNING FOR BASIC FORM

In training bonsai from nursery-grown trees, it is important to remove all but the key branches. These will form the simplified skeleton of the bonsai-to-be, since it is from these limbs that new leaves and new shoots will grow. Foliage masses can be created around each branch if new shoots are pinched back as they develop.

In pruning the five-year-old tree **A**, only one branch is allowed to remain at each level. This avoids the oversymmetrical effect of opposite branches, creates a feeling of openness between branches and accentuates the diminutive trunk. Tree **B**, a distorted specimen such as can occasionally be found in a nursery or growing wild, is pruned mainly to simplify the branch structure and emphasize its asymmetrical trunk. The trees in **C** are a kind one is sometimes fortunate enough to discover: specimens with interesting branch patterns, selectively pruned, are immediately attractive as bonsai.

that are large enough to make the cuts easily, without strain.

Do not leave stubs when removing branches, but do cut just outside the branch collars, at angles equal but opposite to angles of the branch bark ridges.

Cut back to buds, or side branches, when shortening branches.

Don't be too hasty about removing dead wood. Sometimes it is aesthetically useful.

Wiring

Branches and even trunks of bonsai trees can be trained by use of wire, twisted spirally along the areas to be trained. Thus, branches can be bent into desired angles and directions. After several months, remove the wires and branches will stay in their new positions.

Inspect wires frequently during seasons of vigorous growth, lest wires leave unnatural grooves.

When wiring, gentle is the key word — no matter how stubborn a branch may be.

Annealed copper wire of various thicknesses is used by many growers. Ordinary copper wire is readily annealed (made softer) by heating in an oven.

Soft aluminum wire that needs no annealing is also used.

Root Pruning

Root pruning usually goes hand in hand with repotting. Root pruning is necessary whenever a bonsai becomes root-bound in its container. Roots should be checked annually.

A container-grown plant is root-bound when a mass of tightly woven roots cover most or all of the growing medium. Screens over drainage holes, in extreme cases, may be completely covered with roots.

Deciduous species usually require root pruning every two to three years; evergreens, every three to five years.

Root pruning is best done when plants are dormant, before new growth begins.

To root prune, allow the root medium to become moderately dry. Remove the root mass from the container and unravel roots carefully, using fingers and perhaps a cheap dinner fork with tines spread, or a special tool called a root hook.

Then carefully dislodge about one-third of the medium from around the roots.

With sharp pruners or snips, trim roots so that only about an inch of each root extends beyond the remaining medium. Always cut back to a lateral root no matter how tiny.

Then, with fresh medium, repot the bonsai into the same container, or a larger or more artistically desirable one.

PRUNING WITH A
DECORATIVE EYE

Leona Woodring Smith

areful examination before you start pruning can help you find interesting shapes and textures sculpted by nature. Unusual curves and angles resulting from wind, rain and sun can provide indoor beauty for your home.

Leona Woodring Smith, *freelance writer and lecturer, is the author of* **The Forgotten Art of Flower Cookery**. *She and her husband operated Heritage Gardens, a herb and everlasting flower business in Edenton, North Carolina.*

Attractive lines of fallen tree limbs, gnarled roots and twisted branches are being used commercially to display clothing, jewelry and other baubles.

Designers are adding new dimensions of beauty to homes by using the simplicity of natural wood sculpture, perhaps to fill an empty corner, or maybe to sweep one's eyes upward to another level.

Flower arrangers have long depended on the interesting forms of tree branches for basic outlines. Opportunities are endless.

Decorative pruning throughout the year can provide something special in every season — flowering branches in late winter and early spring, green leaves for arranging summer flowers, colorful foliage and berries in the fall and greenery for the Christmas season.

Who hasn't admired a vase filled with sprays of red-berried holly at Christmastime, or lingered over one filled with blooms of forsythia and pussy willows in February while outside there is still snow on the ground?

A truly dedicated decorative pruner may delay cutting of certain branches until a more suitable season for decorating with them.

For example, while pruning in spring, one might postpone cutting an unwanted (on the plant) evergreen branch that would make a perfect background for a summer floral arrangement.

Or, while fall pruning, leave a few well-budded branches of forsythia for spring forcing. Or temporarily spare a wayward holly branch, and prune it later for holiday decorating.

Spring

Forcing flowering and leafing branches indoors can often be accomplished before springtime arrives outdoors. Forcing results will vary, depending upon geographical location, weather and species.

In late winter start checking the bushes and branches for swollen buds. Some of the best woody branches for forcing flowers are: apple, forsythia, plum, birch, lilac, pussy willow, cherry, magnolia, dogwood, redbud, peach, witch hazel and maples (red and silver).

Forced foliage is useful, too. Try branches of willow, privet, buckeye, honeysuckle and other species that leaf out early in spring.

To condition for indoor blooming, crush the base of branches to aid water intake. Place them in a container of warm water and keep in a warm place, but not next to the fireplace, radiator or other heat source, lest buds dry out before opening. Change the water every three or four days.

It may take several days to several weeks, depending upon the time of season and the nature of the branch, but it's a rewarding adventure to watch the new growth unfold.

Summer

Flowers are abundant everywhere in the summer months, begging to brighten any or all rooms in the house.

Since foliage is essential in all flower arrangements, prune with a decorative eye. Deciduous shrubs and evergreens provide greenery for flower arranging, and branches can provide basic outlines. Plan a design, however, before cutting, so precious material will not be wasted.

Branches of graceful cotoneaster, leucothoe, witch hazel or laurel will provide natural curves. Snippings of yew, boxwood or juniper can add fullness to arrangements. Carefully chosen, well-shaped evergreen branches can provide design backgrounds that will last through several changes of floral accents.

Autumn

Fall prunings offer an abundance of decorative material. The variance of tints and tones and smooth and rough textures of an interestingly formed branch can make it a natural sculpture.

Showy fruited branches of pyracantha, bittersweet, beautyberry, leucothoe, cotoneaster, some of the shrub roses, and others provide ready-made bouquets.

Colorful leaves such as maple, oak and beech may be allowed to dry naturally, or preserved with glycerine.

Prunings from wisteria or grapevines can easily be fashioned into handsome wreaths with a little hand-shaping while they are still pliable. In addition to or instead of those, try making wreaths with long flexible shoots of willow, bayberry, fragrant sumac, shrub dogwoods (especially those with red and yellow bark) and others.

Burs (beech), cones (pine, spruce, hemlock, alder), nuts, seed pods (sycamore, golden rain, magnolia) and spurs (apple) may be saved for making wreaths, swags, plaques and various other creations.

Winter

Bringing in one's own greenery can be very satisfying to the home gardener, and not just at holiday time.

Mixed evergreens can make an interesting winter bouquet that will last for months and provide special fragrance.

Branches from broadleaf evergreens such as holly, rhododendron, mountain laurel, magnolia, pieris, cherry laurel and leucothoe should have basal ends of woody stems crushed to aid water absorption, then be placed in buckets of water and kept in a cool place until needed. Small clippings can be sprinkled with water, packed in plastic bags and kept under similar conditions.

Needled evergreens such as fir, hemlock, spruce, pine and others are best clipped closer to the time of use. They, too, require cool, damp storage.

Prunings from ivy (vines or groundcovers) can provide year-round greenery indoors. Gather lots of ivy cuttings (preferably small-leaved) about three inches long and plant a wreath with them by sticking the cuttings into a wire wreath frame packed with moist sphagnum moss, wrapped with thin green plastic. Treated as a house plant, it will last for years.

Wreaths, door swags, kissing balls, roping (white pine shoots are ideal for ropes) and other Christmas decorations can be made in advance, sprinkled with water and stored in plastic bags in a cool, but not freezing, area.

Every time you get out your pruning shears, remember to look for decorative material before you cut. The more you look, the more you will see.

Prune with a decorative eye.

Winter pruning at Brooklyn Botanic Garden.

PRUNING TOOLS

ALAN D. COOK

Pruning tools, like the tools of any craft or profession, must be:

❶ suited to the task; e.g. it is difficult to shear a hedge with a saw;

❷ of sufficient capacity for the task at hand; e.g. pruning shears made for one hand cannot cut through limbs that two-hand loppers can; and

❸ clean, sharp and in good operating order; e.g. a rusty saw with a bent blade is hard to use and makes poor pruning cuts.

What kind of shears to use for various branch sizes (see below) depends somewhat on the species and the condition of the wood. For example, pin oak branches are harder to cut than linden. Dead wood, until decay sets in, is tougher than live wood.

Pruning Shears for One Hand

Various sizes and models of hand pruners are available, in a wide range of prices. The amount of pruning you expect to do will help determine type and quality of pruning shears to buy.

Hand pruning shears are good for branches up to 3/4 inch in diameter if you have a hand that can make a person cringe during a handshake. If you're the person who cringes, hand shears will get you through 1/2-inch branches. Unless your shears are topnotch and heavy duty, attempting to cut larger branches can

ruin them, and strain you.

There are two kinds of hand shears, determined by the way they cut: 1) the snap cut, also called the anvil cut, and 2) the draw cut, also called the scissors action and bypass type. In the first style, a sharpened blade cuts against a broad, grooved blade. In the second, a thin, sharp blade slides closely past a thicker but also sharp blade.

The latter usually costs more, but makes cleaner, closer cuts and is preferred by most serious pruners.

Models are available with swiveling handles to reduce fatigue, and there is at least one model for left-handed persons.

For hands of limited strength due to arthritis, age, youth or other reasons, there is a lightweight rachet-action hand pruner on the market. It is of the anvil cut persuasion, not the best. But it makes reasonable pruning cuts in short, easy steps. It won't make big tough cuts, and the mechanism that holds the blades shut usually breaks sooner or later. Even so, this tool is a boon to many of us.

With hand pruners, there's a danger of the literal manifestation. Keep fingers away so the hand pruners prune limbs, not hands. Any victim will testify that at the last instant one will realize some skin is in the wrong place, but one cannot stop in time. Be careful.

A belt-mounted sheath helps keep

hand pruners handy.

If your pruning shears have a detachable spring between the handles (for returning handles to open, ready-to-cut position after each cut) it is wise to keep an extra spring (order from your dealer) on hand. Such a spring will break eventually, and springless pruners are tedious to use.

Lopping Shears for Two Hands

Lopping shears, usually just called loppers, are available with two handles ranging from 16 inches long or less to huge models with three-foot handles. Other things being equal, the longer the handles, the bigger the branches loppers can cut. Small loppers may do no better than sturdy one-hand pruners, 1/2 to 3/4 inch. Big ones can handle limbs two inches or more in diameter.

As with one-hand shears, loppers come in either snap cut or draw cut style. Rachet-action loppers are also available, and some models feature mechanisms for increased leverage.

With loppers, the larger the cut, the harder it is to do a clean job without tearing bark that should be left intact.

Pruning Knife

Pruning knives have heavy, hooked blades. In the hands of an oldtime gardener or nurseryman, a pruning knife is a precision instrument, swift and beautiful. In the clutches of an average suburbanite, however, such a knife has a diabolical will of its own, apt to be dangerous to both the plant and the operator. Unless you're already a skilled practitioner, forget the pruning knife.

Hedge Shears

Manual hedge shears have long, flat blades and relatively short handles, one for each hand. If you intend to do a lot on hedges or other formal work, get a pair with a shock absorbing device to minimize an aggravation that could be called "pruner's wrist." Heavy duty hedge shears with one serrated blade are best for difficult jobs.

Pruning Saws

There are scores of makes and kinds of pruning saws. Fineness of cutting edge is measured in points (teeth per inch). An eight-point saw is for delicate, close work on small shrubs and young trees. Average saws are about 5-1/2 to 6 points, while 4-1/2 point saws are for fairly heavy limbs.

A rash of new saw designs, mostly from Japan, are on the market. Some have clever triple-edged teeth; some have two opposing rows of teeth. These cut relatively small branches rapidly and well.

One disadvantage is the lack of self-cleaning ability when used on resinous plants, such as conifers. Also, most have thin, somewhat brittle blades. If used with careless energy, blades may snap.

At least one U.S. company is said to be working on stronger blades with fast-cutting teeth.

Handles are important to those with small or not-strong hands. Many saws have a slightly curved handle that fits no normal hand and requires a lumberjack's grip. Pistol grips and "D" grips are easier to handle.

Curved blade or straight? Many prefer a curved blade that cuts on the draw stroke, especially for light to moderate pruning. Some straight blade saws, especially for heavy work, cut on the push stroke.

A double-edge saw has fine teeth on one edge of the blade, coarse on the other. And whoever invented the double-edged saw should have to use one in a densely branched small tree. Can't you guess what the upper edge is likely to do to an upper branch while you're cutting a lower branch?

Bow saws are good only where no

obstruction exists for a foot or more above the area to be cut.

Pole Pruning Tools

Pole-mounted pruners are operated either by a lever that is squeezed or by a lanyard that is pulled. Some employ snap cut and others draw cut mechanisms, as discussed above.

Pole pruning tools are available with wood, metal or synthetic poles. Often they have three six-foot sections that fit together to create a six-, twelve- or eighteen-foot pole. Telescoping poles are also available, too.

Wooden poles are heaviest. Metal poles conduct electricity dangerously well (as from overhead utility wires not noticed until too late). Fiberglass and other plastic poles are light-weight and don't conduct electricity. Of course, even a nonconductive pole or lanyard will entertain a charge of electricity if it is wet.

Never use a pole or other pruning device within ten feet of wires, even if they are "only" low-voltage telephone lines. Unfunny things can happen.

The higher the limb to be pruned, the harder it is to make the cut in proper location and angle.

Poles also can be fitted with pruning saws. But unless the limb to be cut is strong and firmly affixed, the saw bounces with sawing strokes in a frustrating manner.

If the limb is strong and firmly attached, sawing with a pole is easier. But such a limb is likely to be heavy, and dangerous to the pruner standing below. Often the pruning person's best hope is that said limb, after severance, will lodge tenaciously and temporarily safely among remaining branches.

And a saw produces sawdust, which won't put a lump on one's head, but will irritate one's eyes.

However, using a pruning saw is safer than pruning from a ladder, or from atop a small box balanced atop a larger box. Please, prune only when both feet are planted firmly on firm ground.

Pruning Rope

There is a device consisting of a light rope (lanyard) with a flexible section of cutting teeth in the middle. One end of the rope is tossed over an overhead branch and the ends of the rope pulled resolutely back and forth to operate the cutting section.

The above remarks about pole saw safety apply here, too.

Power Pruning Tools

Various pruning tools are powered by electric, gasoline or pneumatic motors.

Usefulness of electric tools is limited by the length of allowable extension cords. Smaller motors must employ shorter cords to avoid excessive voltage drop.

Also, remember that powered cutting tools will sever whatever they are applied to, and electric pruners have been known to cut the cords that feed them.

Gasoline-powered tools are not limited by bothersome cords, but they are noisier, smokier and usually heavier and harder to start than electric units.

Pneumatics run by compressed air and are seldom suitable for amateurs.

Always wear sturdy work shoes and snugly-fitting clothing, including gloves, when operating power tools. Never use electric tools when foliage is wet, including grass underfoot.

Power hedge trimmers are okay, if used with care, for light formal shearing of hedges and topiary figures. They are faster than hand-operated hedge shears, but don't necessarily do as good a job.

Power-driven chain saws, mostly gasoline fueled, dot suburban and even urban landscapes. And persons injured by power saws dot emergency rooms across the land. Most of us should call professionals for work requiring chain saws.

When you disregard that advice and proceed to prune with a chain saw, at least keep both feet on the ground, and cut nothing higher than your waist. Repeat: Most of us should call professionals for work requiring chain saws.

If you use power for pruning, by all means purchase or rent models that require two hands for operation (will shut off if either hand is removed from controls).

Care of Tools

Keep cutting edges sharp. Sharpen cutting edges of drawcut pruners and loppers on the outside edge only, so inside surfaces sliding against one another are left flat. Sharpen cutting edges of snap cut pruners on both sides.

Some handy persons can deftly file edges of saw teeth, but the average person should take saws to a professional sharpener.

Clean tools after each use, or during use on resinous wood. Apply a thin coat of light oil (some use baby oil) on metal surfaces, and oil pivot joints before storing between jobs.

Follow manufacturers' maintenance advice on power tools.

Use tools respectfully. Don't twist or strain pruners or loppers. Long, firm strokes with a saw will cut faster, but if one is too eager the saw tip may wedge in the kerf on a too-rapid push stroke, bending the blade. Or breaking it.

A bent saw is an abomination. Straighten it? Maybe. More likely you'll get two bends instead of one.

Treat wooden handles with linseed oil once a month to preclude splits that punish hands. Or, better, paint handles — wood and metal — bright yellow or orange so you can spot them easily when they try to hide in the grass. 🌲

WHERE TO GET PRUNING TOOLS

AMERICAN STANDARD CO.
P.O. Box 325
Plantsville, CT 06479

AMES LAWN AND GARDEN TOOLS
P.O. Box 1774
Parkersburg, WV 26102

ARBORIST SUPPLY HOUSE
P.O. Box 23607
Ft. Lauderdale, FL 33307

CLAPPER'S
1125 Washington St.
W. Newton, MA 02165

GARDENER'S SUPPLY CO.
128 Intervale Rd.
Burlington, VT 0541-2804

A.M. LEONARD INC.
6665 Spiker Rd.
Piqua, OH 45356

MACKENZIE NURSERY SUPPLY
P.O. Box 322
Perry, OH 44081

MELLINGERS INC.
2310 W. South Range
North Lima, OH 44452-9731

WALTER F. NICKE
Box 433, McCleod Lane
Topsfield, MA 01983

PRUNING GLOSSARY

Arborist — A specialist in planting and transplanting, pruning and diagnosing the ailments of trees and in tree surgery and maintenance.

Branch bark ridge — The darker ridge of bark which forms above the intersection of trunk and branch (see drawing on page 12).

Branch collar — The bulge of growth on the trunk at the base of a branch (see illustration, page 12).

Broadleaf evergreen — An evergreen with wide, flat leaves, such as rhododendron or holly.

Candle — New terminal growth on a pine, from which needles will emerge.

Crotch — The angle formed by a main and secondary branch or by a branch and the trunk.

Deadheading — Removal of flower heads past their prime.

Dehorning — A drastic pruning technique that entails removal of large branches, especially high in the crown. See *Topping*.

Disbudding — Selective removal of flower buds so that the remaining buds receive more of the plant's energy and thus grow larger.

Espalier — A tree or shrub trained in a pattern against a wall or trellis.

Hatracking — Poor tree-pruning technique which usually results in overly long dead ends or stubs.

Heading back — Pruning to shorten branches, often to reduce the size of a tree or shrub.

Lateral branch — A branch attached to and subordinate to another branch or a trunk.

Leader — A trunk or stem extending up through the main axis of a tree or shrub and clearly emerging at the top.

Pinching — Shortening shoots, usually by using one's fingers, to create a bushier, more compact plant.

Pleaching — Intertwining branches of trees or shrubs to form an arbor.

Pollarding — Severe pruning of the main branches of a tree each year to produce a thick growth of young branches.

Scaffold limbs — The principal branches growing from the trunk or other main branch to form the framework of a tree or large shrub.

Stubbing off — See *Hatracking*.

Sucker — A shoot or stem that originates from the roots or trunk beneath or near the ground.

Thinning — Removing entire branches to create a more open plant. This type of pruning accentuates a plant's natural character.

Topping — Indiscriminate cutting off of the tops of large limbs or the trunk of a tree, which results in a stressed, weakened tree.

Watersprouts — Rapidly growing, soft shoots that commonly appear after heavy pruning. They are rarely strongly attached branches and should be removed unless they fill a hole in the tree's framework.